P9-ASF-974
WITHDRAWN
L. R. COLLEGE LIBRARY

A

THE BHAGAVAD GĪTĀ
OR
THE LORD'S SONG

THE BHAGAVAD GĪTĀ
OR
THE LORD'S SONG

TRANSLATED BY

ANNIE BESANT

Third Adyar Edition

Carl A. Rudisill Library
LENOIR RHYNE COLLEGE

1953

THE THEOSOPHICAL PUBLISHING HOUSE

ADYAR, MADRAS, INDIA

Sold by
The Theosophical Press
Wheaton, Illinois

PK
3633
.B5
B5
1953

First Edition:		*London*	*1895*
Second	,,	,,	*1896*
Third	,,	,,	*1903*
Fourth	,,	,,	*1904*
First	,,	*Adyar*	*1939*
Second	,,	,,	*1947*
Third	,,	,,	*1953*

35123
July 1957

(Copyright—all rights reserved)

PRINTED & PUBLISHED IN INDIA.

PUBLISHER'S NOTE

DR. BESANT'S translation of the Bhagavad Gītā is rightly esteemed for its beauty of language, its clarity of expression, and its close adherence to the original Saṁskṛt. Since its first publication in 1895, many reprints in different editions, with and without the Samskrit text, have appeared. In the present edition, we have faithfully adhered to Dr. Besant's work as regards the verbal text, the orthography, and the punctuation. In the latter, we have at two places, in order to start a new paragraph (IX, 33 and XVIII, 58), changed a semi-colon and colon into a full stop.

In the typographical form, however, we have ventured on a new departure. Instead of printing each verse separately, we have taken them together in groups, and printed them accordingly in longer paragraphs. This has the advantage that a particular sequence of thought, running through two or more verses, may be pursued in one continuous flow without being constantly broken up by the eye meeting, at every new verse, blank spaces and new paragraphs. For the same reason the numbering of the verses has been transferred to the margin. We have here and there favoured the isolation of still shorter paragraphs, even of single verses, from a longer context, in order the better to bring out some particularly characteristic, striking, and well-known verses, sometimes also to mark obvious interpolations.

The addition of K. Browning's Index to the Samskrit names, leading ideas and technical terms, first published in 1916, will be fully appreciated, we trust, by the serious student of this storehouse of wisdom of ancient Āryāvarta.

May it then in its new form be of as great help to the Motherland's and to the whole World's spiritual progress as it has been in the past.

In this Second Adyar Edition we have moreover adopted, the scientific system of transliteration well-known in academic circles the world over. In this task the assistance of S'rī H. G. Narahari of the Adyar Library was available to us.

T. P. H.

DEDICATED

TO ALL

ASPIRANTS IN EAST AND WEST

PREFACE

TO THE FIRST EDITION

AMONG the priceless teachings that may be found in the great Hindu poem of the *Mahābhārata*, there is none so rare and precious as this, " The Lord's Song ". Since it fell from the divine lips of S'rī Kṛṣṇa on the field of battle, and stilled the surging emotions of His disciple and friend, how many troubled hearts has it quieted and strengthened, how many weary souls has it led to Him! It is meant to lift the aspirant from the lower levels of renunciation, where objects are renounced, to the loftier heights where desires are dead and where the yogī dwells in calm and ceaseless contemplation, while his body and mind are actively employed in discharging the duties that fall to his lot in life. That the spiritual man need not be a recluse, that union with the divine Life may be achieved and maintained in the midst of worldly affairs, that the obstacles to that union lie not outside us but within us—such is the central lesson of the BHAGAVAD GĪTĀ.

It is a scripture of Yoga; now Yoga is literally union, and it means harmony with the divine Law, the becoming one with the divine Life, by the subdual of all outward-going energies. To reach this, balance must be gained, equilibrium, so that the self, joined to the Self, shall not be affected by pleasure or pain, desire or aversion, or any of the " pairs of opposites " between which untrained selves swing backwards and forwards. Moderation is therefore the key-note of the GĪTĀ, and the harmonizing of all the constituents of man, till they vibrate in perfect attunement with the One, the supreme Self. This is the aim the disciple is to set before him. He must learn not to be attracted by the attractive, nor repelled by the repellent, but must see both as manifestations of the one Lord, so that they may be lessons for his guidance, not fetters for his bondage. In the midst of turmoil he must rest in the Lord of Peace, discharging every duty to the fullest, not because he seeks the results of his actions, but because it is his duty to perform them. His heart is an altar, love to his Lord the flame burning upon it ; all his acts, physical and mental, are sacrifices offered on the altar ; and once offered, he has with them no further concern.

As though to make the lesson more impressive, it was given on a field of battle ; Arjuna, the warrior-prince, was to vindicate his brother's title, to destroy a usurper who was oppressing the land ; it was his duty as prince, as warrior, to fight for the deliverance of his nation and to restore order and peace. To make the contest more bitter, loved comrades and friends stood on both sides, wringing his heart with personal anguish, and making a conflict of duties as well as physical strife.

Could he slay those to whom he owed love and duty, and trample on ties of kindred? To break family ties was a sin; to leave the people in cruel bondage was a sin; where was the right way? Justice must be done, else law would be disregarded; but how slay without sin? The answer is the burden of the book: Have no personal interest in the event; carry out the duty imposed by the position in life; realize that Īśvara, at once Lord and Law, is the doer, working out the mighty evolution that ends in bliss and peace; be identified with Him by devotion, and then perform duty as duty, fighting without passion or desire, without anger or hatred; thus activity forges no bonds, Yoga is accomplished, and the soul is free.

Such is the obvious teaching of this sacred book. But as all the acts of an Avatāra are symbolical, we may pass from the outer to the inner planes, and see in the fight of Kurukṣetra the battlefield of the soul, and in the sons of Dhṛtarāṣṭra enemies it meets in its progress ; Arjuna becomes the type of the struggling soul of the disciple, and S'rī Kṛṣṇa is the Logos of the soul. Thus the teaching of the ancient battlefield gives guidance in all later days, and trains the aspiring soul in treading the steep and thorny path that leads to peace. To all such souls in East and West come these divine lessons, for the path is one, though it has many names, and all souls seek the same goal, though they may not realize their unity.

In order to preserve the precision of the Samskṛt, a few technical terms have been given in the original in foot notes; Manas is the mind, both in the lower mental processes in which it is swayed by the senses, by passions and emotions, and in the higher processes of reasoning; Buddhi is the faculty above the ratiocinating mind, and is the Pure Reason, exercising the discriminative faculty of intuition, of spiritual discernment; if these original words are not known to the reader, the BHAGAVAD-GĪTĀ loses much of its practical value as a treatise on Yoga, and the would-be learner becomes confused.

The epithets applied to S'rī Kṛṣṇa and Arjuna—the variety of which is so characteristic of Samskṛt conversation—are for the most part left untranslated, as being musical they thus add to the literary charm, whereas the genius of English is so different from that of Samskṛt, that the many-footed epithets become sometimes almost grotesque in translation. Names derived from that of an ancestor, as Pārtha, meaning the son of Pṛitha, Kaunteya, meaning the son of Kuntī, are used in one form or the other, according to the rhythm of the sentence. One other trifling matter, which is yet not trifling if it aids the student: when Ātmā means the One Self, the SELF of all, it is printed in small capitals; where it means the lower, the personal self, it is printed in ordinary type; this is done because there is sometimes a play on the word, and it is difficult for an untrained reader to follow the meaning without some such assistance. The word Brahman, the ONE, the Supreme, is throughout translated "the ETERNAL". The word "Deva," literally "Shining One" is thus translated throughout. The use of the western word "God" alike for "Brahman" and for the "Devas" is most misleading; the Hindu never uses the one for the other, and never blurs the unity of the Supreme by the multiplicity of ministering Intelligences.

My wish, in adding this translation to those already before the public, was to preserve the spirit of the original, especially in its deeply devotional tone, while at the same time giving an accurate translation, reflecting the strength and the terseness of the Samskṛt. In order that mistakes, due to my imperfect knowledge, might be corrected, the first and second editions of this translation passed through the hands of one or other of the following gentlemen—friends of mine at Benares—to whom I here tender my grateful acknowledgments: Bābus Pramada Dās Mitra, Ganganāth Jhā, Kāli Charan Mitra, and Upendranāth Basu. A few of the notes are also due to them. In the third and fourth editions I have also been much helped by Bābu Bhagavān Dās, to whom I add my cordial thanks.

ANNIE BESANT

FIRST DISCOURSE

Dhritarashtra said :

1 On the holy plain, on the field of Kuru,[1] gathered together, eager for battle, what did they, O Sañjaya, my people and the Pāṇḍavas ?

Sanjaya said :

2 Having seen arrayed the army of the Pāṇḍavas, the Prince Duryodhana approached his teacher,[2] and spake these words :

3 " Behold this mighty host of the sons of Pāṇḍu, O teacher, arrayed by

[1] The common ancestor for the contending parties, the Kurus and Pāṇḍavas, in the impending battle.

[2] Droṇa, the son of Bharadvāja.

the son of Drupada, thy wise disciple.
4 Heroes are these, mighty bowmen,
to Bhīma and Arjuna equal in battle;
Yuyudhāna, Virāṭa and Drupada of the
5 great car:[1] Dhṛṣṭaketu, Cekitāna and
the valiant King of Kās'ī, Purujit
and Kuntibhoja, and S'aivya, bull[2]
6 among men; Yudhāmanyu the strong,
and Uttamaujas the brave; Saubhadra
and the Draupadeyas,[3] all of great cars.
7 Know further all those who are our
chiefs, O best of the twice-born, the
leaders of my army; these I name
8 to thee for thy information: Thou,

[1] One able to fight alone ten thousand bowmen.

[2] The bull, as the emblem of manly strength and vigour, is often used as an epithet of honour.

[3] Abhimanyu, the son of Subhadrā and Arjuna, and the sons and grandsons of Drupada.

Lord, and Bhīṣma, and Karṇa and
Kṛpa, conquering in battle; As'vat-
thāman, Vikarṇa, and Saumadatti[1]
9 also; and many others, heroes, for my
sake renouncing their lives, with diverse
weapons and missiles and all well-skilled
10 in war. Yet insufficient seems this
army of ours, though marshalled by
Bhīṣma, while that army of theirs
seems sufficient, though marshalled by
11 Bhīma;[2] therefore in the rank and
file let all, standing firmly in their res-
pective divisions, guard Bhīṣma, even
all ye Generals."

[1] The son of Somadatta.

[2] The commentators differ in their interpretation of this verse: Ānandagiri takes it to mean just the reverse of S'ridhara Svāmi, "aparyāptam" being taken by the one as "insufficient," by the other as "unlimited".

12 To enhearten him, the Ancient of
the Kurus, the Grandsire,[1] the glorious, blew his conch, sounding on high
13 a lion's roar. Then conches and
kettledrums, tabors and drums and
cow-horns, suddenly blared forth, and
14 the sound was tumultuous. Then,
stationed in their great war-chariot,
yoked to white horses, Mādhava[2] and
the son of Pāṇḍu[3] blew their divine
15 conches, Pāñcajanya by Hṛṣīkes'a, and Devadatta by Dhanañjaya.[4]

[1] Bhīṣma.

[2] S'rī Kṛṣṇa.

[3] Arjuna.

[4] Pāñcajanya, S'rī Kṛṣṇa's conch, was made from the bones of the giant Pañcajana, slain by Him. The title Hṛṣikes'a is "Lord of the senses". Dhanañjaya, the "conqueror of wealth," is a title often given to Arjuna, whose conch is the "God-given".

Vṛkodara[1] of terrible deeds, blew his
16 mighty conch, Pauṇḍra; the King
Yudhiṣṭhira, the son of Kuntī, blew
Anantavijaya; Nakula and Sahadeva,
17 Sughoṣa and Maṇipuṣpaka[2], and
Kāshya,[3] of the great bow, and S'ik-
haṇḍī, the mighty car-warrior, Dhṛs-
ṭadyumna and Virāṭa and Sātyakī, the
18 unconquered. Drupada and the Draupadeyas, O Lord of earth, and Saubhadra, the mighty-armed, on all sides
19 their several conches blew. That
tumultuous uproar rent the hearts of

[1] Bhīma; the meaning of the name of his conch is doubtful.

[2] The conches of the remaining three brothers were named respectively "endless victory," "honey-tone," and "jewel-blossom".

[3] The King of Kās'ī, the modern Benares.

the sons of the Dhṛtarāṣṭra, filling the
earth and sky with sound.
20 Then, beholding the sons of Dhṛtarāṣṭra standing arrayed, and the flight
of missiles about to begin, he whose
crest is an ape, the son of Pāṇḍu, took
21 up his bow, and spake this word to
Hṛṣīkes'a, O Lord of earth :

Arjuna said:

In the midst, between the two armies,
22 stay my chariot, O Acyuta,[1] that I
may behold these standing, longing for
battle, with whom I must strive in this
23 outbreaking war, and gaze on those
here gathered together, ready to fight,
desirous of pleasing in battle the evil-
minded son of Dhṛtarāṣṭra.

[1] The changeless, the immovable.

24 Sanjaya said :

Thus addressed by Guḍākes'a,[1] Hṛṣīkes'a, O Bhārata, having stayed that
best of chariots in the midst, between
25 the two armies, over against Bhīṣma,
Droṇa and all the rulers of the world,
said : " O Pārtha, behold these Kurus
26 gathered together." Then saw Pārtha
standing there, uncles and grandfathers,
teachers, mother's brothers, cousins,
27 sons and grandsons, comrades, fathers-
in-law and benefactors also in both
armies ; seeing all these kinsmen thus
28 standing arrayed, Kaunteya,[2] deeply
moved to pity, thus uttered in sad-
ness :

[1] The lord of sleep, Arjuna.

[2] The son of Kuntī, Arjuna.

Arjuna said:

Seeing these my kinsmen, O Kṛṣṇa,
29 arrayed, eager to fight, my limbs fail
and my mouth is parched, my body
quivers, and my hair stands on end,
30 Gāṇḍīva slips from my hand, and my
skin burns all over. I am not able to
31 stand, my mind is whirling, and I see
adverse omens, O Keśava.[1] Nor do I
foresee any advantage from slaying
32 kinsmen in battle. For I desire not
victory, O Kṛṣṇa, nor kingdom, nor
pleasures; what is kingdom to us, O
Govinda, what enjoyment, or even life?
33 Those for whose sake we desire kingdom, enjoyments and pleasures, they

[1] "He who has luxurious hair," or, "He who sleeps on the waters".

stand here in battle, abandoning life
34 and riches—teachers, fathers, sons, as
well as grandfathers, mother's brothers,
fathers-in-law, grandsons, brothers-in-
35 law, and other relatives. These I do
not wish to kill, though myself slain, O
Madhusūdana,[1] even for the sake of the
kingship of the three worlds; how then
36 for earth? Slaying these sons of Dhṛtarāṣṭra, what pleasure can be ours, O
Janārdana?[2] Killing these desperadoes,
37 sin will but take hold of us. Therefore
we should not kill the sons of Dhṛtarāṣṭra, our relatives; for how, killing
our kinsmen, may we be happy, O
Mādhava?

[1] The slayer of Madhu, a demon.

[2] "Destroyer of the people." S'ri Kṛṣṇa as the warrior conquering all forms of evil.

38 Although these, with intelligence
overpowered by greed, see no guilt in
the destruction of a family, no crime in
39 hostility to friends, why should not
we learn to turn away from such a sin,
O Janārdana, who see the evils in the
40 destruction of a family? In the destruction of a family the immemorial
family traditions[1] perish; in the
perishing of tradition, lawlessness
41 overcomes the whole family; owing
to predominance of lawlessness, O
Kṛṣṇa, the women of the family
become corrupt; women corrupted

[1] Dharma: this is a wide word, primarily meaning the essential nature of a thing, that which makes it to be what it is externally; hence, the laws of its being, its duty; and it includes religious rites, appropriate to those laws, customs, also righteousness.

O Vārṣneya,[1] there ariseth caste-con-
42 fusion; this confusion draggeth to hell
the slayers of the family, and the family;
for their ancestors fall, deprived of
43 riceballs and libations. By these caste-
confusing misdeeds of the slayers of the
family, the everlasting caste customs[2]
44 and family customs[2] are abolished. The
abode of the men whose family customs
are extinguished, O Janārdana, is ever-
lastingly in hell. Thus have we heard.
45 Alas! in committing a great sin are we
engaged, we who are endeavouring to
kill our kindred from greed of the
46 pleasures of kingship. If the sons of
Dhṛtarāṣṭra, weapon-in-hand, should

[1] Belonging to the family of Vṛṣṇi.

[2] Dharma.

slay me, unresisting, unarmed, in the battle, that would for me be the better.

47 **Sanjaya said:**

Having thus spoken on the battle-field, Arjuna sank down on the seat of the chariot, casting away his bow and arrow, his mind overborne by grief.

Thus in the glorious Upaniṣads of the BHAGAVAD-GĪTĀ, the science of the ETERNAL, the scripture of Yoga, the dialogue between Śri Kṛṣṇa and Arjuna, the first discourse, entitled:

THE DESPONDENCY OF ARJUNA

SECOND DISCOURSE

1 **Sanjaya said:**

To him thus with pity overcome, with smarting brimming eyes, despondent, Madhusūdana spake these words:

2 **The Blessed Lord said:**

Whence hath this dejection befallen thee in this perilous strait, ignoble,[1] heaven-closing,[2] infamous, O Arjuna?
3 Yield not to impotence, O Pārtha! it doth not befit thee. Shake off this paltry faint-heartedness! Stand up, Parantapa![3]

[1] Literally, un-āryan.

[2] Literally, non-svargan: cowardice in the warrior closed on him the door of Svarga, heaven.

[3] Conqueror of foes.

4 **Arjuna said:**
How, O Madhusūdana, shall I attack
Bhīṣma and Droṇa with arrows in
battle, they who are worthy of rever-
5 ence, O slayer of foes? Better in this
world to eat even the beggar's crust
than to slay these most noble Gurus.
Slaying these Gurus, our well-wishers,[1]
I should taste of blood-besprinkled
6 feasts. Nor know I which for us be
the better, that we conquer them or
they conquer us—these, whom having
slain we should not care to live, even
these arrayed against us, the sons of
7 Dhṛtarāṣṭra. My heart is weighed

[1] More often translated, "desirous of wealth," but the word is used elsewhere for well-wisher, "desirous of good," and the term is more in accordance with the tone of Arjuna's remarks.

down with the vice of faintness; my
mind is confused as to duty.[1] I ask
Thee which may be the better—that
tell me decisively. I am Thy disciple,
8 suppliant to Thee; teach me. For I
see not that it would drive away this
anguish that withers up my senses, if
I should attain unrivalled monarchy on
earth, or even the sovereignty of the
Shining Ones.

9 **Sanjaya said:**

Gudākes'a, conqueror of his foes,
having thus addressed Hṛṣīkes'a, and
said to Govinda, "I will not fight!"
10 became silent. Then Hṛṣīkes'a,
smiling, as it were, O Bhārata, spake

[1] Dharma.

these words to him, despondent, in the
midst of the two armies.

11 **The Blessed Lord said:**

Thou grievest for those that should
not be grieved for, yet speakest words
of wisdom.[1] The wise grieve neither
12 for the living nor for the dead. Nor at
any time verily was I not, nor thou, nor
these princes of men, nor verily shall
13 we ever cease to be, hereafter. As the
dweller in the body experienceth in the
body childhood, youth, old age, so
passeth he on to another body; the
14 steadfast one grieveth not thereat. The
contacts of matter, O son of Kuntī,
giving cold and heat, pleasure and pain,

[1] Words that sound wise, but miss the deeper sense of wisdom.

they come and go, impermanent; en-
15 dure them bravely, O Bhārata. The
man whom these torment not, O chief
of men, balanced in pain and pleasure,
steadfast, he is fitted for immortality.
16 The unreal hath no being; the real
never ceaseth to be; the truth about
both hath been perceived by the
seers of the Essence of things.[1]
17 Know THAT to be indestructible by
whom all this is pervaded. Nor can
any work the destruction of that
18 imperishable One. These bodies of
the embodied One, who is eternal,
indestructible and immeasurable, are
known as finite. Therefore fight, O
Bhārata.

[1] Tattva.

19 He who regardeth this[1] as a slayer,
and he who thinketh he is slain, both
of them are ignorant. He slayeth not,
20 nor is he slain; he is not born, nor
doth he die; nor having been, ceaseth
he any more to be; unborn, perpetual,
eternal and ancient, he is not slain
21 when the body is slaughtered. Who
knoweth him indestructible, perpetual,
unborn, undiminishing, how can that
man slay, O Pārtha, or cause to be
22 slain? As a man, casting off worn-out
garments, taketh new ones, so the
dweller in the body, casting off worn-
out bodies, entereth into others that
23 are new. Weapons cleave him not, nor
fire burneth him, nor waters wet him,

[1] The dweller in the body.

24 nor wind drieth him away. Uncleav-
able he, incumbustible he, and indeed
neither to be wetted nor dried away;
perpetual, all-pervasive, stable, immov-
25 able, ancient, unmanifest, unthinkable, immutable, he is called; therefore
knowing him as such, thou shouldst
26 not grieve. Or if thou thinkest of him
as being constantly born and constantly
dying, even then, O mighty-armed,
27 thou shouldst not grieve. For certain
is death for the born, and certain is
birth for the dead; therefore over the
inevitable, thou shouldst not grieve.
28 Beings are unmanifest in their origin,
manifest in their midmost state, O
Bhārata, unmanifest likewise are they
in dissolution. What room then for

29 lamentation? As marvellous one regardeth him; as marvellous another speaketh thereof; as marvellous another
heareth thereof; yet having heard,
30 none indeed understandeth. This
dweller in the body of everyone is ever
invulnerable, O Bhārata; therefore
thou shouldst not grieve for any
creature.

31 Further, looking to thine own duty[1]
thou shouldst not tremble; for there is
nothing more welcome to a Kṣattriya[2]
32 than righteous war. Happy the Kṣāt-
triyas, O Pārtha, who obtain such a
fight, offered unsought as an open door
33 to heaven. But if thou wilt not carry

[1] Dharma.

[2] A person of the second, the warrior, caste.

on this righteous warfare, then casting
away thine own duty[1] and thine
34 honour, thou wilt incur sin. Men will
recount the perpetual dishonour, and,
to one highly esteemed, dishonour
35 exceedeth death. The great car-war-
riors[2] will think thee fled from the
battle from fear, and thou, that wast
highly thought of by them, wilt be
36 lightly held. Many unseemly words
will be spoken by thine enemies, slan-
dering thy strength; what more painful
37 than that? Slain, thou wilt obtain
heaven; victorious, thou wilt enjoy the
earth; therefore stand up, O son of
38 Kuntī, resolute to fight. Taking as

[1] Dharma.

[2] The generals.

equal pleasure and pain, gain and loss, victory and defeat, gird thou for the battle; thus thou shalt not incur sin.

39 This teaching set forth to thee is in
accordance with the Sāṅkhya[1]; hear it
now according to the Yoga[2], imbued
with which teaching, O Pārtha, thou
shall cast away the bonds of action.
40 In this there is no loss of effort, nor
is there transgression. Even a little of
this knowledge[3] protects from great
41 fear. The determinate Reason[4] is but

[1] One of the six systems of Indian philosophy, dealing with evolution.

[2] Another of the same systems, dealing with meditation.

[3] Dharma.

[4] Buddhi.

onepointed, O joy of the Kurus; many-
branched and endless are the thoughts
42 of the irresolute. Flowery speech is
uttered by the foolish, rejoicing in the
letter of the Vedas,[1] O Pārtha, saying:
43 "There is naught but this"; with
desire for self,[2] with heaven for goal,
they offer birth as the fruit of action,
and prescribe many and various ceremonies for the attainment of pleasure
44 and lordship. For them who cling to
pleasure and lordship, whose minds are
captivated by such teaching, is not
designed this determinate Reason,[3] on

[1] The Hindu Scriptures.

[2] Those whose very self is desire, Kāma, and who therefore act with a view to win heaven and also rebirth to wealth and rank.

[3] Buddhi.

45 contemplation [1] steadily bent.[2] The Vedas deal with the three attributes;[3] be thou above these three attributes, O Arjuna; beyond the pairs of opposites, ever steadfast in purity,[4] careless of

[1] Samādhi, the third state of consciousness in meditation.

[2] The following alternative translation of s'lokas 42, 43, and 44 is offered: "The flowery speech that the unwise utter, O Pārtha, clinging to the word of the Veda, saying there is nothing else, ensouled by desire and longing after heaven, (the speech) that offereth only rebirth as the (ultimate) fruit of action, that is full of (recommendations to) various rites for the sake of (gaining) enjoyments and sovereignty—the thought of those misled by that (speech), cleaving to pleasures and lordship not being inspired with resolution, is not engaged in contemplation." This is closer to the original, which is all in one sentence.

[3] Guṇas=attributes, or forms of energy. They are Sattva, rhythm, harmony, or purity; Rajas, motion, activity, or passion; Tamas, inertia, darkness, or stupidity.

[4] Sattva.

46 possessions, full of the SELF. All the
Vedas are as useful to an enlightened
Brāhmaṇa[1] as is a tank in a place
covered all over with water.
47 Thy business is with the action only,
never with its fruits; so let not the
fruit of action be thy motive, nor be
48 thou to inaction attached. Perform
action, O Dhanañjaya, dwelling in union
with the divine,[2] renouncing attachments, and balanced evenly in success
and failure: equilibrium is called yoga.
49 Far lower than the Yoga of Discrimination[3] is action, O Dhanañjaya.

[1] A person of the highest, the priestly and teaching, caste.

[2] Dwelling in yoga, union.

[3] Union with Buddhi, the innermost sheath (or vehicle) of Ātmā.

Take thou refuge in the Pure Reason[1];
pitiable are they who work for fruit.
50 United to the Pure Reason[1] one
abandoneth here both good and evil
deeds; therefore cleave thou to yoga;
51 yoga is skill in action. The Sages,
united to the Pure Reason,[1] renounce
the fruit which action yieldeth, and,
liberated from the bonds of birth, they
52 go to the blissful seat. When thy
mind[1] shall escape from this tangle of
delusion, then thou shalt rise to in-
difference as to what has been heard
53 and shall be heard. When thy
mind,[1] bewildered by the Scriptures[2],
shall stand immovable, fixed in

[1] Buddhi.
[2] Sruti.

contemplation, then shalt thou attain unto yoga.[1]

54 **Arjuna said:**

What is the mark of him who is stable of mind,[2] steadfast in contemplation, O Kes'ava? how doth the stable-minded[3] talk, how doth he sit, how walk?

55 **The Blessed Lord said:**

When a man abandoneth, O Pārtha, all the desires of the heart,[4] and is satisfied in the SELF by the SELF, then is
56 he called stable in mind.[2] He whose

[1] To union with Ātmā, the SELF; yoga implies harmony with the divine will. The word translated contemplation is, as before, Samādhi.

[2] Prajñā.

[3] Dhī.

[4] Manas.

mind[1] is free from anxiety amid pains, indifferent amid pleasures, loosed from passion, fear and anger, he is called a
57 sage[2] of stable mind.[3] He who on every side is without attachments, whatever hap of fair and foul, who neither likes nor dislikes, of such a one the understanding[4] is well-poised.
58 When, again, as a tortoise draws in on all sides its limbs, he withdraws his senses from the objects of sense, then is his understanding[4] well-poised.

[1] Manas.

[2] A Muni, *i.e.*, a saint or ascetic; in its original meaning one who observed the vow of silence.

[3] Dhi.

[4] Prajñā.

59 The objects of sense, but not the
relish for them,[1] turn away from an
abstemious dweller in the body; and
even relish turneth away from him after
60 the Supreme is seen. O son of Kuntī,
the excited senses of even a wise man,
though he be striving, impetuously
61 carry away his mind.[2] Having restrained them all, he should sit harmonized, I his supreme goal; for whose
senses are mastered, of him the under-
62 standing[3] is well-poised. Man, musing
on the objects of sense, conceiveth an
attachment to these; from attachment

[1] The objects turn away when rejected, but still desire for them remains; even desire is lost when the Supreme is seen.

[2] Manas.

[3] Prajñā.

ariseth desire; from desire anger[1]
63 cometh forth; from anger proceedeth
delusion; from delusion confused memory; from confused memory the destruction of Reason[2]; from destruction
of Reason he perishes.
64 But the disciplined self, moving
among sense-objects with senses free
from attraction and repulsion, mastered
65 by the SELF, goeth to Peace. In that
Peace the extinction of all pains ariseth
for him, for of him whose heart[3] is
peaceful the Reason[4] soon attaineth
66 equilibrium. There is no Pure Reason[4]

[1] Krodha.

[2] Buddhi, here implying specially Discrimination.

[3] Cetas.

[4] Buddhi.

for the non-harmonized, nor for the
non-harmonized is there concentration [1];
for him without concentration there is
no peace, and for the unpeaceful how
67 can there be happiness? Such of the
roving senses as the mind [2] yieldeth to,
that hurries away the understanding,[3]
just as the gale hurries away a ship
68 upon the waters. Therefore, O mighty-
armed, whose senses are all completely
restrained from the objects of sense,
of him the understanding [3] is well-
poised.

69 That which is the night of all beings,
for the disciplined man is the time of

[1] Bhāvana.
[2] Manas.
[3] Prajñā.

waking, when other beings are waking, then is it night for the sage who seeth.[1]

70 He attaineth Peace, into whom all desires flow as rivers flow into the ocean, which is filled with water, but remaineth unmoved—not he who
71 desireth desires. Whoso forsaketh all desires and goeth onwards free from yearnings, selfless and without
72 egoism—he goeth to Peace. This is the ETERNAL state, O son of Pṛthā. Having attained thereto none is bewildered. Who, even at the

[1] The Sage is awake to things over which the ordinary man sleeps, and the eyes of the Sage are open to truths shut out from the common vision, while *vice versa* that which is real for the masses is illusion for the Sage.

death-hour, is established therein, he goeth to the Nirvāṇa of the ETERNAL.

Thus in the glorious Upaniṣads of the BHAGAVAD-GĪTĀ, the science of the ETERNAL, the scripture of Yoga, the dialogue between S'ri Kṛṣṇa and Arjuna, the second discourse, entitled

YOGA: BY THE SAṄKHYA

THIRD DISCOURSE

Arjuna said :

1 If it be thought by Thee that knowledge is superior to action, O Janārdana, why dost Thou, O Keśava, enjoin on
2 me this terrible action ? With these perplexing words Thou only confusest my understanding[1]; therefore tell me with certainty the one way by which I may reach bliss.

3 **The Blessed Lord said :**

In this world there is a twofold path, as I before said, O sinless one : that of yoga by knowledge, of the Sāṅkhyas;

[1] Buddhi.

and that of yoga by action, of the
4 Yogīs. Man winneth not freedom from
action by abstaining from activity, nor
by mere renunciation doth he rise to
5 perfection. Nor can anyone, even for
an instant, remain really actionless;
for helplessly is everyone driven to
action by the qualities[1] born of nature.[2]
6 Who sitteth, controlling the organs of
action, but dwelling in his mind[3] on
the objects of the senses, that bewild-
7 ered man is called a hypocrite. But
who, controlling the senses by the
mind[3], O Arjuna, with the organs of
action without attachment, performeth

[1] Guṇas.
[2] Prakṛti.
[3] Manas.

8 yoga by action[1], he is worthy. Perform thou right[2] action, for action is
superior to inaction, and, inactive,
even the maintenance of thy body
9 would not be possible. The world is
bound by action, unless performed for
the sake of sacrifice; for that sake, free
from attachment, O son of Kuntī, perform thou action.

10 Having in ancient times emanated mankind together with sacrifice, the Lord of emanation[3] said: "By this shall ye propagate; be this to you the

[1] Karma-Yoga is the consecration of physical energy on the divine Altar; *i.e.*, the using of one's organs of action simply in service, in obedience to Law and Duty.

[2] Regulated, prescribed as a duty; or regularly.

[3] Prajāpati.

11 giver of desires[1]; with this nourish ye
the Shining Ones, and may the Shining
Ones nourish you; thus nourishing one
another, ye shall reap the supremest
12 good. For nourished by sacrifice, the
Shining Ones shall bestow on you the
enjoyments you desire." A thief verily
is he who enjoyeth what is given by
Them without returning Them aught.
13 The righteous, who eat the remains of
the sacrifice, are freed from all sins;
but the impious, who dress food for
their own sakes, they verily eat sin.
14 From food creatures become; from
rain is the production of food; rain
proceedeth from sacrifice; sacrifice

[1] Kāmadhuk, the cow of Indra, from which each could milk what he wished for; hence the giver of desired objects.

ariseth out of action. Know thou that
15 from Brahma [1] action groweth, and
Brahma from the Imperishable cometh.
Therefore the ETERNAL, the all-per-
meating, is ever present in sacrifice.
16 He who on earth doth not follow
the wheel thus revolving, sinful of life
and rejoicing in the senses, he, O son
17 of Pṛthā, liveth in vain. But the man
who rejoiceth in the SELF, with the
SELF is satisfied, and is content in
the SELF, for him verily there is noth-
18 ing to do; for him there is no interest
in things done in this world, nor any in
things not done, nor doth any object of
19 his depend on any being. Therefore,

[1] An Indian of much knowledge translates Brahma here as "the Vedas".

without attachment, constantly perform action which is duty, for, by performing action without attachment
man verily reacheth the Supreme.
20 Janaka and others indeed attained to
perfection by action; then having an
eye to the welfare of the world also,
21 thou shouldst perform action. Whatsoever a great man doeth, that other
men also do; the standard he setteth
up, by that the people go.
22 There is nothing in the three worlds,
O Pārtha, that should be done by Me,
nor anything unattained that might
be attained; yet I mingle in action.
23 For if I mingled not ever in action
unwearied, men all around would follow
24 My path, O son of Pṛthā. These worlds

would fall into ruin, if I did not perform action; I should be the author of confusion of castes, and should destroy these creatures.
25 As the ignorant act from attachment to action, O Bhārata, so should the wise act without attachment, desiring
26 the welfare of the world. Let no wise man unsettle the mind of ignorant people attached to action; but acting in harmony with Me let him render all
27 action attractive. All actions are wrought by the qualities[1] of nature only. The self, deluded by egoism,[2]
28 thinketh: "I am the doer." But he, O mighty-armed, who knoweth the

[1] Guṇas.

[2] Ahamkāra, the separate "I am."

essence of the divisions of the qualities and functions, holding that "the qualities move amid the qualities,"[1] is
29 not attached. Those deluded by the qualities of nature are attached to the functions of the qualities. The man of perfect knowledge should not unsettle the foolish whose knowledge is imperfect.
30 Surrendering all actions to Me, with thy thoughts resting on the supreme SELF, from hope and egoism freed, and of mental fever cured, engage in battle.
31 Who abide ever in this teaching of

[1] The Guṇas, qualities, as sense-organs move amid the Guṇas, qualities, as sense-objects. A suggested reading is "The functions dwell in the propensities." S'aṅkarācārya says, "of the class of qualities and the class of actions"; or the arrangement or relations of qualities and actions.

Mine, full of faith and free from cavil-
ling, they too are released from actions.
32 Who carp at My teaching and act not
thereon, senseless, deluded in all knowledge, know thou these mindless ones
as fated to be destroyed.
33 Even the man of knowledge behaves
in conformity with his own nature;
beings follow nature; what shall re-
34 straint avail? Affection and aversion
for the objects of sense abide in the
senses; let none come under the domi-
nion of these two; they are obstructors
35 of the path. Better one's own duty,[1]
though destitute of merit, than the
duty[1] of another, well-discharged.
Better death in the discharge of one's

[1] Dharma.

own duty; [1] the duty [1] of another is full of danger.

Arjuna said:

36 But dragged on by what does a man commit sin, reluctantly indeed, O Vārṣ-
ṇeya, as it were by force constrained?

The Blessed Lord said:

37 It is desire, it is wrath, begotten by the quality of motion; [2] all-consuming,
all-polluting, know thou this as our foe
38 here on earth. As a flame is enveloped by smoke, as a mirror by dust, as an
embryo is wrapped by the amnion, so
39 This [3] is enveloped by it. Enveloped

[1] Dharma.
[2] Rajas.
[3] The universe: "This" as opposed to "THAT," the ETERNAL. Some say "This" stands for "knowledge".

is wisdom by this constant enemy of the
wise in the form of desire, which is
40 insatiable as a flame. The senses, the
mind[1] and the Reason[2] are said to be
its seat; by these enveloping wisdom it
bewilders the dweller in the body.
41 Therefore, O best of the Bhāratas,
mastering first the senses, do thou slay
this thing of sin, destructive of wisdom
42 and knowledge. It is said that the
senses are great; greater than the senses is the mind[1]; greater than the
mind[1] is the Reason[2]; but what is
43 greater than the Reason[2], is HE[3]. Thus
understanding Him as greater than the

[1] Manah.
[2] Buddhi.
[3] The Supreme.

Reason[1], restraining the self by the SELF, slay thou, O mighty-armed, the enemy in the form of desire, difficult to overcome.

Thus in the glorious Upaniṣads of the BHAGAVAD-GĪTĀ, the science of the ETERNAL, the scripture of Yoga, the dialogue between S'rī Kṛṣṇa and Arjuna, third discourse, entitled :

THE YOGA OF ACTION

[1] Buddhi.

FOURTH DISCOURSE

1 **The Blessed Lord said:**

This imperishable yoga I declared to
Vivasvān; Vivasvān taught it to Manu;
2 Manu to Ikṣvāku told it. This, hand-
ed on down the line, the King-Sages
knew. This yoga by great efflux of
time decayed in the world, O Parantapa.
3 This same ancient yoga hath been to-
day declared to thee by Me, for thou
art My devotee and My friend; it is the
supreme Secret.

4 **Arjuna said:**

Later was Thy birth, earlier the
birth of Vivasvān; how then am I to

understand that Thou declaredst it in the beginning?

5 **The Blessed Lord said:**

Many births have been left behind by Me and by thee, O Arjuna. I know them all, but thou knowest not thine,
6 O Parantapa. Though unborn, the imperishable SELF, and also the Lord of all beings brooding over nature, which is Mine own, yet I am born
7 through My own Power[1]. Whenever there is decay of righteousness[2], O Bhārata, and there is exaltation of

[1] Māyā, the power of thought that produces form, which is transient and therefore unreal compared with the eternal Reality; hence Māyā comes to be taken as the power of producing illusion.

[2] Dharma.

unrighteousness[1], then I Myself come
8 forth; for the protection of the good,
for the destruction of evil-doers, for the
sake of firmly establishing righteous-
9 ness[2], I am born from age to age. He
who thus knoweth My divine birth and
action, in its essence, having abandoned
the body, cometh not to birth again,
10 but cometh unto Me, O Arjuna. Freed
from passion, fear and anger, filled with
Me, taking refuge in Me, purified in the
fire[3] of wisdom, many have entered
11 into My Being. However men approach
Me, even so do I welcome them, for

[1] Adharma, the opposite of Dharma, all that is disorderly, against the nature of things.

[2] Dharma.

[3] Tapas, from tap, blazing like fire.

the path men take from every side is
Mine, O Pārtha.
12 They who long after success in action
on earth worship the Shining Ones;
for in brief space verily, in this world
13 of men, success is born of action. The
four castes were emanated by Me, by
the different distribution of qualities[1]
and actions; know Me to be the author
of them, though the actionless and
14 inexhaustible. Nor do actions affect
Me, nor is the fruit of action desired by
Me. He who thus knoweth Me is not
15 bound by actions. Having thus known,
our forefathers, ever seeking liberation,
performed action; therefore do thou

[1] Guṇas.

also perform action, as did our forefathers in the olden time.
16 "What is action, what inaction?"
Even the wise are herein perplexed.
Therefore I will declare to thee the
action by knowing which thou shalt be
17 loosed from evil. It is needful to discriminate action, to discriminate unlawful action, and to discriminate inaction;
18 mysterious is the path of action. He
who seeth inaction in action, and action
in inaction, he is wise among men, he is
harmonious, even while performing all
19 action. Whose works are all free from
the moulding of desire, whose actions
are burned up by the fire of wisdom,
20 him the wise have called a Sage. Having abandoned attachment to the fruit

of action, always content, nowhere
seeking refuge, he is not doing any-
21 thing, although doing actions. Hoping
for naught, his mind and self controlled,
having abandoned all greed, performing
action by the body alone, he doth not
22 commit sin. Content with whatsoever
he obtaineth without effort, free from
the pairs of opposites, without envy,
balanced in success and failure, though
23 acting he is not bound. Of one with
attachment dead, harmonious, with his
thoughts established in wisdom, his
works sacrifices, all action melts away.
24 The ETERNAL the oblation, the
ETERNAL the clarified butter, are
offered in the ETERNAL the fire by the
ETERNAL; unto the ETERNAL verily

shall he go who in his action meditateth
25 wholly upon the ETERNAL.[1] Some
Yogīs offer up sacrifice to the Shining
Ones[2]; others sacrifice only by pouring
sacrifice into the fire of the ETERNAL.
26 Some pour as sacrifice hearing and the
other senses into the fires of restraint;
some pour sound and the other objects
of sense into the fires of the senses
27 as sacrifice; others again into the
wisdom-kindled fire of union attained
by self-control, pour as sacrifice all the
functions of the senses and the functions
28 of life; yet others the sacrifice of wealth,
the sacrifice of austerity, the sacrifice

[1] He who sees the ETERNAL beneath the transitory alone goes to the ETERNAL; all others remain bound in the world of forms.

[2] Literally divine sacrifice.

of yoga, the sacrifice of silent reading
and wisdom, men concentrated and of
29 effectual vows; yet others pour as
sacrifice the outgoing breath in the
incoming, and the incoming in the
outgoing, restraining the flow of the outgoing and incoming breaths, solely
absorbed in the control of breathing;[1]
30 others, regular in food, pour as sacrifice their life-breaths in life-breaths.
All these are knowers of sacrifice,
and by sacrifice have destroyed their
31 sins. The eaters of the life-giving[2] remains of sacrifice go to the changeless

[1] Prāṇāyāma, restraint of breath, a technical name for this practice.

[2] Amṛta: it is the elixir of immortality, and the amṛta-remains, therefore, are foods that give immortality.

ETERNAL. This world is not for the
non-sacrificer, much less for the other, O
32 best of the Kurus. Many and various
sacrifices are thus spread out before the
ETERNAL[1]. Know thou that all these
are born of action, and thus knowing
thou shalt be free.
33 Better than sacrifice of any objects
is the sacrifice of wisdom, O Parantapa. All actions in their entirety,
34 O Pārtha, culminate in wisdom. Learn
thou this by discipleship,[2] by investi-
gation, and by service. The wise,
the seers of the essence of things, will
35 instruct thee in wisdom. And having
known this, thou shalt not again fall

[1] "In the Vedas" is another interpretation.

[2] Literally, falling at the feet, *i.e.*, the feet of the teacher.

into this confusion, O Pāṇḍava; for
by this thou wilt see all beings without
exception in the SELF, and thus in Me.
36 Even if thou art the most sinful of
all sinners, yet shalt thou cross over
37 all sin by the raft of wisdom. As
burning fire reduces fuel to ashes, O
Arjuna, so doth the fire of wisdom
38 reduce all actions to ashes. Verily
there is no purifier in this world like
wisdom; he that is perfected in yoga
finds it in the SELF in due season.
39 The man who is full of faith[1] obtaineth
wisdom, and he also who hath mastery
over his senses; and, having obtained
wisdom, he goeth swiftly to the su-
40 preme Peace. But the ignorant, faithless,

[1] Who is intent upon faith.

doubting self goeth to destruction; nor this world, nor that beyond, nor happiness, is there for the doubting
41 self. He who hath renounced actions by yoga, who hath cloven asunder doubt by wisdom, who is ruled by the SELF[1], actions do not bind him, O
42 Dhanañjaya. Therefore, with the sword of the wisdom of the SELF cleaving asunder this ignorance-born doubt, dwelling in thy heart, be established in yoga. Stand up, O Bhārata.

Thus in the glorious Upaniṣads of the BHAGAVAD-GĪTĀ, the science of the ETERNAL, the scripture of Yoga, the dialogue between S'rī Kṛṣṇa and Arjuna, the fourth discourse, entitled:

THE YOGA OF WISDOM

[1] Madhusūdana explains *ātmavantam* as "always watchful".

FIFTH DISCOURSE

1 **Arjuna said :**

Renunciation of actions Thou praisest, O Kṛṣṇa, and then also yoga. Of the two which one is the better ? That tell me conclusively.

2 **The Blessed Lord said :**

Renunciation and yoga by action both lead to the highest bliss ; of the two, yoga by action is verily
3 better than renunciation of action. He should be known as a perpetual ascetic [1], who neither hateth nor desireth ; free from the pairs of opposites, O mighty-armed, he is easily set free

[1] Saṁnyāsi ; one who renounces all.

4 from bondage. Children, not Sages,
speak of the Sāṅkhya[1] and the Yoga[2] as
different; he who is duly established
in one obtaineth the fruits of both. That
5 place which is gained by the Sāṅkhyas
is reached by the Yogīs also. He seeth,
who seeth that the Sāṅkhya and the Yoga
6 are one. But without yoga, O mighty-
armed, renunciation is hard to attain
to; the yoga-harmonized Muni swiftly
goeth to the ETERNAL.

7 He who is harmonized by yoga,
self-purified, SELF-ruled, the senses subdued, whose SELF is the SELF of
all beings, although acting he is not
8 affected. "I do not anything," should

[1] See footnote page 42.

[2] *Ibid.*

think the harmonized one, who knoweth
the essence of things; seeing, hearing,
touching, smelling, eating, moving,
9 sleeping, breathing, speaking, giving,
grasping, opening and closing the eyes,
he holdeth: "The senses move among
10 the objects of the senses." He who
acteth, placing all actions in the ETERNAL,
abandoning attachment, is unaffected
by sin as a lotus leaf by the
11 waters. Yogīs, having abandoned attachment,
perform action only by the
body, by the mind [1], by the Reason [2],
and even by the senses, for the purification
12 of the self. The harmonized
man, having abandoned the fruit of

[1] Manas.

[2] Buddhi.

action, attaineth to the eternal Peace;
the non-harmonized, impelled by desire,
13 attached to fruit, are bound. Mentally
renouncing all actions, the sovereign
dweller in the body resteth serenely in
the nine-gated city[1], neither acting nor
causing to act.

14 The Lord of the world produceth
not the idea of agency, nor actions, nor
the union together of action and its
fruit; nature, however, manifesteth.
15 The Lord accepteth neither the evil-
doing nor yet the well-doing of any.
Wisdom is enveloped by unwisdom;
16 therewith mortals are deluded. Verily,
in whom unwisdom is destroyed by the

[1] The body, often called the city of the ETERNAL.

wisdom of the SELF, in them wisdom, shining as the sun, reveals the Supreme.
17 Thinking on THAT, merged in THAT, established in THAT, solely devoted to THAT, they go whence there is no return, their sins dispelled by wisdom.
18 Sages look equally on a Brāhmaṇa, adorned with learning and humility, a cow, an elephant, and even a dog and
19 an outcaste.[1] Even here on earth everything is overcome by those whose mind[2] remains balanced; the ETERNAL is incorruptible and balanced; therefore they are established in the ETERNAL.
20 With Reason[3] firm, unperplexed, the

[1] A S'vapāka, the lowest class of outcastes.
[2] Manas.
[3] Buddhi.

knower of the ETERNAL, established
in the ETERNAL, neither rejoiceth on
obtaining what is pleasant, nor sorrow-
eth on obtaining what is unpleasant.
21 He, whose self is unattached to
external contacts and findeth joy in
the SELF, having the self harmonized
with the ETERNAL by yoga, enjoys
imperishable bliss.

22 The delights that are contact-born,
they are verily wombs of pain, for they
have beginning and ending, O Kaunteya; not in them may rejoice the
23 wise. He who is able to endure here
on earth, ere he be liberated from the
body, the force born from desire and
passion, he is harmonized, he is a happy
24 man. He who is happy within, who

rejoiceth within, who is illuminated
within, that Yogī, becoming the ETER-
NAL, goeth to the Peace[1] of the ETER-
25 NAL. Ṛṣis, their sins destroyed, their
duality removed, their selves controlled,
intent upon the welfare of all beings,
obtain the Peace[1] of the ETERNAL.
26 The Peace[1] of the ETERNAL lies near
to those who know themselves, who are
disjoined from desire and passion, subdued in nature, of subdued thoughts.
27 Having external contacts excluded,
and with gaze fixed between the eye-
brows; having made equal the outgoing
and ingoing breaths moving within the
28 nostrils, with senses, mind,[2] and

[1] Nirvāṇa.
[2] Manas.

Reason [1], ever controlled, solely pursuing
liberation, the Sage, having for ever
cast away desire, fear and passion,
29 verily is liberated. Having known Me,
as the Enjoyer of sacrifice and of
austerity, the mighty Ruler of all the
worlds, and the Lover of all beings, he
goeth to Peace.

Thus in the glorious Upaniṣads of the BHAGAVAD-GĪTĀ, the science of the ETERNAL, the scripture of Yoga, in the dialogue between Srī Kṛṣṇa and Arjuna, the fifth discourse, entitled :

THE YOGA OF
THE RENUNCIATION OF ACTION

[1] Buddhi.

SIXTH DISCOURSE

1 **The Blessed Lord said:**

He that performeth such action as
is duty, independently of the fruit of
action, he is an ascetic[1], he is a Yogī,
not he that is without fire, and without
2 rites. That which is called renunciation
know thou that as yoga, O Pāṇḍava;
nor doth any one become a Yogī with
3 the formative will[2] unrenounced. For
a Sage who is seeking Yoga, action is
called the means; for the same Sage,

[1] The ascetic, the Saṁnyāsī, lights no sacrificial fire, and performs no sacrifices nor ceremonies; but merely to omit these, without true renunciation, is not to be a real ascetic.

[2] Saṅkalpa, the imaginative faculty that makes plans for the future.

when he is enthroned in yoga, serenity
4 is called the means. When a man
feeleth no attachment either for the
objects of sense or for actions, renouncing
the formative will,[1] then, he is
said to be enthroned in yoga.
5 Let him raise the self by the SELF
and not let the self become depressed;
for verily is the SELF the friend of the
self, and also the SELF the self's
6 enemy; the SELF is the friend of the
self of him in whom the self by the
SELF is vanquished; but to the unsubdued
self[2] the SELF verily becometh
7 hostile as an enemy. The higher Self
of him who is SELF-controlled and

[1] Saṅkalpa.
[2] Literally, the non-self.

peaceful is uniform in cold and heat,
pleasure and pain, as well as in honour
8 and dishonour. The Yogī[1] who is satisfied with wisdom and knowledge, unwavering,[2] whose senses are subdued, to
whom a lump of earth, a stone and gold
are the same, is said to be harmonized.
9 He who regards impartially lovers,
friends, and foes, strangers, neutrals,
foreigners and relatives, also the righteous and unrighteous, he excelleth.
10 Let the Yogī constantly engage himself in yoga, remaining in a secret place
by himself, with thought and self sub-
11 dued, free from hope and greed. In a

[1] The word Yogī is used for any one who is practising yoga, as well as for the man who has attained union.

[2] Literally, rock-seated.

pure place, established on a fixed seat of his own, neither very much raised nor very low, made of a cloth, a black antelope skin, and kuśa grass, one
12 over the other, there, having made the mind[1] one-pointed, with thought and the functions of the senses subdued, steady on his seat, he should practise yoga for the purification of the self.
13 Holding the body, head, and neck erect, immovably steady, looking fixedly at the point of the nose, with unseeing
14 gaze, the self serene, fearless, firm in the vow of the Brahmacāri[2], the mind[1] controlled, thinking on Me, harmonized,

[1] Manas.

[2] A Brahmacārī is a man who is keeping the vow of continence, a celibate.

15 let him sit aspiring after Me. The
Yogī, ever united thus with the SELF,
with the mind[1] controlled, goeth to
Peace, to the supreme Bliss[2] that abideth
in Me.
16 Verily yoga is not for him who eateth
too much, nor who abstaineth to excess,
nor who is too much addicted to sleep,
nor even to wakefulness, O Arjuna.
17 Yoga killeth out all pain for him who
is regulated in eating and amusement,
regulated in performing actions, re-
18 gulated in sleeping and waking. When
his subdued thought is fixed on the
SELF, free from longing after all desir-
able things, then it is said, "he is

[1] Manas.
[2] Nirvāṇa.

19 harmonized." As a lamp in a windless
place flickereth not, to such is likened
the Yogī of subdued thought, absorbed
in the yoga of the SELF.

20 That in which the mind finds rest,
quieted by the practice of yoga; that
in which he, seeing the SELF by the
21 SELF, in the SELF is satisfied; that
in which he findeth the supreme delight
which the Reason[1] can grasp beyond the
senses, wherein established he moveth
22 not from the Reality; which having
obtained, he thinketh there is no greater
gain beyond it; wherein established, he
is not shaken even by heavy sorrow;
23 that should be known by the name of
yoga, this disconnection from the union

[1] Buddhi.

with pain. This yoga must be clung to
with a firm conviction and with undesponding mind.[1]

24 Abandoning without reserve all desires born of the imagination[2], by the
mind[3] curbing in the aggregate of the
25 senses on every side, little by little let
him gain tranquillity, by means of Reason[4] controlled by steadiness; having
made the mind[3] abide in the SELF, let
26 him not think of anything. As often
as the wavering and unsteady mind[3]
goeth forth, so often reining it in, let
him bring it under the control of the
27 SELF. Supreme joy is for this Yogī

[1] Cetas.

[2] Saṅkalpa.

[3] Manas.

[4] Buddhi.

whose mind[1] is peaceful, whose passion-
nature is calmed, who is sinless and of
28 the nature of the ETERNAL. The
Yogī who thus, ever harmonizing the
self, hath put away sin, he easily enjoyeth the infinite bliss of contact with
the ETERNAL.
29 The self, harmonized by yoga, seeth
the SELF abiding in all beings, all beings
in the SELF; everywhere he seeth the
30 same. He who seeth Me everywhere,
and seeth everything in Me, of him will
I never lose hold, and he shall never
31 lose hold of Me. He who, established
in unity, worshippeth Me, abiding in
all beings, that Yogī liveth in Me, what-
32 ever his mode of living. He who,

[1] Manas.

through the likeness of the SELF,[1] O Arjuna, seeth equality in everything, whether pleasant or painful, he is considered a perfect Yogī.

33 **Arjuna said :**

This yoga which Thou hast declared to be by equanimity, O Madhusūdana,
I see not a stable foundation for it,
34 owing to restlessness; for the mind[2] is verily restless, O Kṛṣṇa; it is impetuous, strong and difficult to bend. I deem it as hard to curb as the wind.

35 **The Blessed Lord said :**

Without doubt, O mighty-armed, the mind[2] is hard to curb and restless; but

[1] The same SELF shining in the heart of each.

[2] Manas.

it may be curbed by constant practice
36 and by dispassion. Yoga is hard to
attain, methinks, by a self that is uncontrolled; but by the SELF-controlled
it is attainable by properly directed
energy.

37 **Arjuna said:**

He who is unsubdued but who possesseth faith, with the mind[1] wandering away from yoga, failing to attain
perfection in yoga, what path doth he
38 tread, O Kṛṣṇa? Fallen from both,
is he destroyed like a rent cloud, unsteadfast, O mighty-armed, deluded in
39 the path of the ETERNAL? Deign, O
Kṛṣṇa, to completely dispel this doubt

[1] Manas.

of mine; for there is none to be
found save Thyself able to destroy
this doubt.

40 **The Blessed Lord said:**

O son of Pṛthā, neither in this world
nor in the life to come is there destruction for him; never doth any who
worketh righteousness, O beloved, tread
41 the path of woe. Having attained to
the worlds of the pure-doing, and having
dwelt there for immemorial years,
he who fell from yoga is reborn in a
42 pure and blessed house; or he may
even be born into a family of wise
Yogīs; but such a birth as that is most
43 difficult to obtain in this world. There
he recovereth the characteristics belonging to his former body, and with

these he again laboureth for perfection,
44 O joy of the Kurus. By that former
practice he is irresistibly swept away.
Only wishing to know yoga, even
the seeker after yoga goeth beyond
45 the Brāhmic word;[1] but the Yogī,
labouring with assiduity, purified from
sin, fully perfected through manifold
births, he reacheth the supreme
goal.

46 The Yogī is greater than the ascetics; he is thought to be greater than even the wise; the Yogī is greater than the men of action; therefore become thou
47 a Yogī, O Arjuna! and among all
Yogīs, he who full of faith, with the
inner SELF abiding in Me, adoreth Me,

[1] The Vedas.

he is considered by Me to be the most completely harmonized.

Thus in the glorious Upaniṣads of the BHAGAVAD-GĪTĀ, the science of the ETERNAL, the scripture of Yoga, in the dialogue between Srī Kṛṣṇa and Arjuna, the sixth discourse, entitled :

THE YOGA OF SELF-SUBDUAL

SEVENTH DISCOURSE

1 **The Blessed Lord said:**

With the mind[1] clinging to me, O
Pārtha, performing yoga, refuged in
Me, how thou shalt without doubt
know Me to the uttermost, that hear
2 thou. I will declare to thee this knowledge and wisdom in its completeness,
which, having known, there is nothing
more here needeth to be known.

3 Among thousands of men scarce one
striveth for perfection; of the success-
ful strivers scarce one knoweth Me in
4 essence. Earth, water, fire, air, ether,

[1] Manas.

Carl A. Rudisill Library
LENOIR RHYNE COLLEGE

Mind,[1] and Reason[2] also and Egoism[3]
—these are the eightfold division of
5 My nature.[4] This the inferior.

Know My other nature[4], the higher,
the life-element, O mighty-armed, by
6 which the universe is upheld. Know
this to be the womb of all beings. I
am the source of the forthgoing of the
whole universe and likewise the place
7 of its dissolving. There is naught
whatsoever higher than I, O Dhanañjaya. All this is threaded on Me, as
rows of pearls on a string.

[1] Manas.

[2] Buddhi.

[3] Ahaṅkāra.

[4] Prakṛti, matter in the widest sense of the term, including all that has extension. The "Higher Prakṛti," of the next verse, is sometimes called Daivīprakṛti, the Light of the Logos.

8 I the sapidity in waters, O son of
Kuntī, I the radiance in moon and
sun; the Word of Power[1] in all the
Vedas, sound in ether, and virility in
9 men; the pure fragrance of earths and
the brilliance in fire am I; the life in
all beings am I, and the austerity in
10 ascetics. Know Me, O Pārtha! as the
eternal seed of all beings. I am the
Reason[2] of the Reason[2]-endowed, the
11 splendour of splendid things am I. And
I the strength of the strong, devoid of
desire and passion. In beings I am
desire not contrary to duty[3], O Lord
of the Bhāratas.

[1] The Praṇava, the Om.

[2] Buddhi.

[3] Dharma.

12 The natures that are harmonious,
active, slothful [1], these know as from
Me; not I in them, but they in Me.
13 All this world, deluded by these natures
made by the three qualities,[2] knoweth
not Me, above these, imperishable.
14 This divine illusion [3] of Mine caused
by the qualities,[2] is hard to pierce;
they who come to Me, they cross over
15 this illusion.[3] The evil-doing, the deluded, the vilest men, they come not to
Me, they whose wisdom is destroyed by

[1] Sāttvic, rājasic, tāmasic, that is, those in whom one of the three qualities, Sattva, Rajas, Tamas predominates.

[2] Guṇas.

[3] Māyā.

illusion[1], who have embraced the nature of demons.[2]

16 Fourfold in division are the righteous ones who worship me, O Arjuna: the suffering, the seeker for knowledge, the self-interested and the wise, O Lord
17 of the Bhāratas. Of these the wise constantly harmonized, worshipping the One, is the best; I am supremely dear to the wise, and he is dear to Me.
18 Noble are all these, but I hold the wise as verily Myself; he, SELF-united is
19 fixed on Me, the highest Path. At the close of many births the man full of wisdom cometh unto Me; "Vāsudeva[3]

[1] Māyā.

[2] Asuras, the opponents of the Suras, or angels.

[3] A name for S'ri Kṛṣṇa, as the son of Vāsudeva.

is all," saith he, the Mahātmā, very
difficult to find.
20 They whose wisdom hath been rent
away by desires go forth to other Shining Ones, resorting to various external
observances, according to their own
21 natures. Any devotee who seeketh to
worship with faith any such aspect, I
verily bestow the unswerving faith of
22 that man. He, endowed with that faith,
seeketh the worship of such a one, and
from him he obtaineth his desires, I
23 verily decreeing the benefits; finite
indeed the fruit; that belongeth to
those who are of small intelligence. To
the Shining Ones go the worshippers
of the Shining Ones, but my devotees
come unto Me.

24 Those devoid of Reason[1] think of
Me, the unmanifest, as having manifestation, knowing not My supreme
nature, imperishable, most excellent.
25 Nor am I of all discovered, enveloped
in My creation-illusion.[2] This deluded
world knoweth Me not, the unborn, the
26 imperishable. I know the beings that
are past, that are present, that are to
come, O Arjuna, but no one knoweth
27 Me. By the delusion of the pairs of opposites, sprung from attraction and repulsion, O Bhārata, all beings walk this
universe wholly deluded, O Parantapa.
28 But those men of pure deeds, in whom
sin is come to an end, they, freed from

[1] Buddhi.
[2] Yoga-Māyā, the creative power of Yoga, all things being the thought-forms of the One.

the delusive pairs of opposites, worship
29 Me, steadfast in vows. They who refuged in Me strive for liberation from birth and death, they know the ETERNAL, the whole SELF-knowledge, and
30 all action. They who know Me as the knowledge of the elements, as that of the Shining Ones, and as that of the Sacrifice[1] they, harmonized in mind, know Me verily even in the time of forthgoing.[2]

Thus in the glorious Upaniṣads of the BHAGAVAD-GĪTĀ, the science of the ETERNAL, the scripture of Yoga, the dialogue between S'ri Kṛṣṇa and Arjuna, the seventh discourse, entitled :

THE YOGA OF DISCRIMINATIVE KNOWLEDGE

[1] These six terms are: Brahman, Adhyātma, Karma, Adhibhūta, Adhidaiva, Adhiyajña.

[2] Death—going forth from the body.

EIGHTH DISCOURSE

1 **Arjuna said:**

What is that ETERNAL,[1] what SELF-knowledge,[2] what Action,[3] O Puruṣottama? And what is declared to be the knowledge of the Elements,[4] what is called the knowledge of the Shining
2 Ones?[5] What is the knowledge of Sacrifice[6] in this body, and how, O Madhusūdhana? And how, at the time of

[1] Brahman.
[2] Adhyātma.
[3] Karma.
[4] Adhibhūta.
[5] Adhidaiva.
[6] Adhiyajña.

forthgoing art Thou known by the SELF-controlled ?

The Blessed Lord said :

3 The indestructible, the supreme is
the ETERNAL;[1] His essential nature is
called SELF-knowledge;[2] the emanation that causes the birth of beings is
4 named Action;[3] Knowledge of the Elements[4] concerns My perishable nature,
and knowledge of the Shining Ones[5]
concerns the life-giving energy;[6] the

[1] Brahman.

[2] Adhyātma.

[3] Karma.

[4] Adhibūta.

[5] Adhidaiva.

[6] Puruṣa, the male creative energy. The supreme Puruṣa is the Divine Man, the manifested God.

knowledge of Sacrifice[1] tells of Me, as wearing the body, O best of living beings.

5 And he who, casting off the body, goeth forth thinking upon Me only at the time of the end, he entereth into My being; there is no doubt of that.
6 Whosoever at the end abandoneth the
body, thinking upon any being, to that
being only he goeth, O Kaunteya, ever
7 to that conformed in nature. Therefore at all times think upon Me only,
and fight. With mind[2] and Reason[3]
set on Me, without doubt thou shalt
8 come to me. With the mind[4] not

[1] Adhiyajña.
[2] Manas.
[3] Buddhi.
[4] Cetas.

wandering after aught else, harmonized by continual practice, constantly meditating, O Pārtha, one goeth to the Spirit supreme, divine.

He who thinketh upon the Ancient, the Omniscient, the All-Ruler, minuter than the minute, the supporter of all, of form unimaginable, refulgent as the
10 sun beyond the darkness, in the time
of forthgoing, with unshaken mind,[1]
fixed in devotion, by the power of yoga
drawing together his life-breath in the
centre of the two eye-brows, he goeth
11 to this Spirit, supreme, divine. That
which is declared indestructible by the Veda-knowers, that which the controlled and passion-free enter, that

[1] Manas.

desiring which Brahmacaryā[1] is performed, that path I will declare to thee
with brevity.
12 All the gates[2] closed, the mind con-
fined in the heart, the life-breath fixed
in his own head, concentrated by yoga,
13 "Om!" the one-syllabled ETERNAL,
reciting, thinking upon Me, he who
goeth forth, abandoning the body, he
14 goeth on the highest path. He who
constantly thinketh upon Me, not thinking ever of another, of him I am easily
reached, O Pārtha, of this ever-har-
15 monized Yogī. Having come to Me,
these Mahātmās come not again to
birth, the place of pain, non-eternal;

[1] The vow of continence.

[2] The gates of the body, *i.e.*, the sense-organs.

they have gone to the highest bliss.
16 The worlds, beginning with the world
of Brahmā, they come and go, O
Arjuna; but he who cometh unto me,
O Kaunteya, he knoweth birth no more.
17 The people who know the day of
Brahmā, a thousand ages[1] in duration,
and the night, a thousand ages in
18 ending, they know day and night. From
the unmanifested all the manifested
stream forth at the coming of day; at
the coming of night they dissolve, even
19 in That called the unmanifested. This
multitude of beings, going forth repeatedly, is dissolved at the coming of
night; by ordination, O Pārtha, it
streams forth at the coming of day.

[1] Yugas.

20 Therefore verily there existeth, higher
than that unmanifested, another unmanifested, eternal, which, in the destroying of all beings, is not destroyed.
21 That unmanifested, "the Indestructible," It is called; It is named the
highest Path. They who reach It
return not. That is My Supreme abode.
22 He, the highest Spirit[1], O Pārtha, may
be reached by unswerving devotion to
Him alone, in whom all beings abide,
by whom all This[2] is pervaded.
23 That time wherein going forth Yogīs
return not, and also that wherein going
forth they return, that time shall I

[1] Puruṣa.

[2] This, the universe, in opposition to THAT, the source of all.

declare to thee, O Prince of the
24 Bhāratas. Fire, light, day-time, the
bright fornight, the six months of the
northern path [1]—then, going forth, the
men who know the ETERNAL go to the
25 ETERNAL. Smoke, night-time, the
dark fortnight also, the six months of
the southern path [1]—then the Yogī,
obtaining the moonlight [2], returneth.
26 Light and darkness, these are thought
to be the world's everlasting paths; by
the one he goeth who returneth not, by
the other he who returneth again.
27 Knowing these paths, O Pārtha, the
Yogī is nowise perplexed. Therefore
in all times be firm in yoga, O Arjuna.

[1] Of the sun.

[2] The lunar, or astral body. Until this is slain the soul returns to birth.

28 The fruit of meritorious deeds, attached in the Vedas to sacrifices, to austerities, and also to almsgiving, the Yogī passeth all these by having known this, and goeth to the supreme and ancient Seat.

Thus in the glorious Upaniṣads of the BHAGAVAD-GĪTĀ, the science of the ETERNAL, the scripture of Yoga, the dialogue between S'rī Kṛṣṇa and Arjuna, the eighth discourse, entitled :

THE YOGA OF THE INDESTRUCTIBLE SUPREME ETERNAL

NINTH DISCOURSE

1 **The Blessed Lord said:**

To thee, the uncarping, verily shall I declare this profoundest Secret, wisdom with knowledge combined, which having known, thou shalt be freed from evil.

2 Kingly Science, kingly Secret, supreme
Purifier, this; intuitional, according to
righteousness[1], very easy to perform,
3 imperishable. Men without faith in this
knowledge[1], O Parantapa, not reaching
Me, return to the paths of this world of
death.

4 By Me all this world is pervaded in My unmanifested aspect; all beings

[1] Dharma.

have root in Me, I am not rooted in
5 them. Nor have beings root in Me;
behold my sovereign Yoga! The support of beings yet not rooted in beings,
6 My SELF their efficient cause. As the
mighty air everywhere moving is rooted
in the ether[1], so all beings rest rooted in
Me—thus know thou.
7 All beings, O Kaunteya, enter my
lower nature[2] at the end of a world-
age[3]; at the beginning of a world-age[3]
8 again I emanate them. Hidden in
nature[2], which is mine own, I emanate
again and again all this multitude of
beings, helpless, by the force of nature[2].

[1] Ākās'a.

[2] Prakṛti.

[3] Kalpa, a period of activity, of manifestation.

9 Nor do these works bind me, O Dhanañjaya, enthroned on high, unattached to
10 actions. Under Me as supervisor nature [1]
sends forth the moving and unmoving:
because of this, O Kaunteya, the universe revolves.

11 The foolish disregard Me, when clad
in human semblance, ignorant of My
supreme nature, the great Lord of
12 beings; empty of hope, empty of deeds,
empty of wisdom, senseless, partaking
of the deceitful, brutal and demoniacal
nature.[2]

[1] Prakṛti.

[2] Prakṛti. The tāmasic Guṇa, or the dark quality of Prakṛti, characterizes the beings here spoken of as rākṣasic and āsuric. Rākṣasas were semi-human beings, brutal and bloodthirsty. Asuras were the opponents of the Devas.

13 Verily the Mahātmas, O Pārtha, partaking of My divine nature[1], worship with
unwavering mind,[2] having known Me,
14 the imperishable source of beings. Always magnifying Me, strenuous, firm in
vows, prostrating themselves before Me,
they worship Me with devotion, ever
harmonized.

15 Others also, sacrificing with the
sacrifice of wisdom, worship Me as the
One and the Manifold everywhere
16 present. I the oblation ; I the sacrifice ;
I the ancestral offering ; I the fire-
giving herb ; the mantram I ; I also the
butter ; I the fire ; the burnt-offering
17 I ; I the Father of this universe, the

[1] Prakṛti.
[2] Manas.

Mother, the Supporter, the Grandsire,
the Holy One to be known, the Word
of Power[1], and also the Ṛk, Sāma, and
18 Yajus[2], The Path, Husband, Lord, Wit-
ness, Abode, Shelter, Lover, Origin,
Dissolution, Foundation, Treasure-
19 house, Seed imperishable. I give heat;
I hold back and send forth the rain;
immortality and also death, being and
non-being[3] am I, Arjuna.
20 The knowers of the three[2], the Soma-
drinkers, the purified from sin, worshipping Me with sacrifice, pray of Me the
way to heaven; they, ascending to the
holy world of the Ruler of the Shining

[1] Omkāra, the sacred Word, Om.

[2] The three Vedas.

[3] Sat and Asat, the final pair of opposites, beyond which is only the One.

21 Ones, eat in heaven the divine feasts of
the Shining Ones. They, having enjoyed the spacious heaven-world, their
holiness withered[1], come back to this
world of death. Following the virtues
enjoined by the three[2], desiring desires,
they obtain the transitory.

22 To those men who worship Me alone,
thinking of no other, to those ever har-
23 monious, I bring full security. Even
the devotees of other Shining Ones,
who worship full of faith, they also
worship Me, O son of Kuntī, though
24 contrary to the ancient rule. I am indeed the enjoyer of all sacrifices, and
also the Lord, but they know Me not

[1] The fruit of their good deeds finished, their reward exhausted.

[2] Vedas.

25 in essence, and hence they fall. They
who worship the Shining Ones go to
the Shining Ones; to the Ancestors[1]
go the Ancestor-worshipper; to the
Elementals[2] go those who sacrifice to
Elementals; but My worshippers come
unto Me.
26 He who offereth to Me with devotion
a leaf, a flower, a fruit, water, that I
accept from the striving self, offered as
27 it is with devotion. Whatsoever thou
doest, whatsoever thou eatest, whatsoever thou offerest; whatsoever thou
28 givest, whatsoever thou doest of austerity, O Kaunteya, do thou that as an
offering unto Me. Thus shalt thou be

[1] Pitṛs.
[2] Bhūtas, Elementals or nature-spirits.

liberated from the bonds of action,
yielding good and evil fruits; thyself
harmonized by the yoga of renunciation, thou shalt come unto Me when
set free.
29 The same am I to all beings; there
is none hateful to me nor dear. They
verily who worship Me with devotion,
are in me, and I also in them.
30 Even if the most sinful worship Me,
with undivided heart, he too must
be accounted righteous, for he hath
31 rightly resolved; speedily he becometh
dutiful and goeth to eternal peace, O
Kaunteya, know thou for certain that
32 My devotee perisheth never. They
who take refuge with Me, O Pārtha,
though of the womb of sin, women,

Vais'yas,[1] even S'ūdras,[2] they also
33 tread the highest Path. How much
rather then holy Brāhmaṇas and devoted royal saints.

Having obtained this transient joyless
34 world, worship thou Me. On Me fix
thy mind[3]; be devoted to Me; sacrifice to Me; prostrate thyself before Me; harmonized thus in the SELF, thou shalt come unto Me, having Me as thy supreme goal.

Thus in the glorious Upaniṣads of the BHAGAVAD-GĪTĀ, the science of the ETERNAL, the scripture of Yoga, the dialogue between S'rī Kṛṣṇa and Arjuna, the ninth discourse, entitled:

THE YOGA OF THE KINGLY SCIENCE AND THE KINGLY SECRET

[1] The third, the merchant, caste.

[2] The fourth, the labouring class.

[3] Manas.

TENTH DISCOURSE

1 **The Blessed Lord said :**

Again, O mighty-armed, hear thou My supreme word, that, desiring thy welfare, I will declare to thee who art beloved.

2 The multitude of the Shining Ones,
or the great Ṛṣis,[1] know not My forth-
coming, for I am the beginning of all
the Shining Ones and the great Ṛṣis.
3 He who knoweth Me, unborn, beginningless, the great Lord of the world,

[1] A Ṛṣi is a man who has completed his human evolution, but who remains in the superphysical regions in touch with the earth, in order to help humanity.

he, among mortals without delusion, is
liberated from all sin.

4 Reason[1], wisdom, non-illusion, forgiveness, truth, self-restraint, calmness,
pleasure, pain, existence, non-existence,
5 fear, and also courage, harmlessness,
equanimity, content, austerity, almsgiving, fame and obloquy are the various
characteristics of beings issuing from
6 Me. The seven great Ṛṣis, the ancient
Four,[2] and also the Manus,[3] were born
of My nature and mind; of them
7 this race was generated. He who

[1] Buddhi.

[2] The four Kumāras, or Virgin Youths, the highest in the Occult Hierarchy of this earth.

[3] The heads and legislators of a race.

knows in essence that sovereignty and
yoga of Mine, he is harmonized by un-
faltering yoga ; there is no doubt there-
8 of, I am the Generator of all ; all evolves
from Me ; understanding thus, the wise
9 adore Me in rapt emotion. Mindful of
Me, their life hidden in Me, illumining
each other, ever conversing about Me,
10 they are content and joyful. To these,
ever harmonious, worshipping in love,
I give the yoga of discrimination[1] by
11 which they come unto Me. Out of
pure compassion for them, dwelling
within their SELF, I destroy the
ignorance-born darkness by the shining
lamp of wisdom.

[1] Buddhi-Yoga.

12 **Arjuna said:**
Thou art the supreme ETERNAL, the
supreme Abode, the supreme Purity,
eternal, divine man, primeval Deity,
13 unborn, the Lord! All the Ṛṣis have
thus acclaimed Thee, as also the divine
Ṛṣi, Nārada; so Asita, Devala, and
Vyāsa; and now Thou Thyself tellest
14 it me. All this I believe true that
Thou sayest to me, O Kes'ava. Thy
manifestation, O Blessed Lord, neither
Shining Ones nor Dānavas[1] com-
15 prehend. Thyself indeed knowest Thyself by Thyself O Puruṣottama!
Source of beings, Lord of beings,
Shining One of Shining Ones, Ruler of
16 the world! Deign to tell without

[1] Demigods, in the Greek sense.

reserve of Thine own divine glories, by
which glories Thou remainest, per-
17 vading these worlds. How may I know
thee, O Yogī, by constant meditation ?
In what, in what aspects art Thou to
be thought of by me, O blessed Lord ?
18 In detail tell me again of Thy yoga
and glory, O Janārdana ; for me there
is never satiety in hearing Thy life-
giving words.

19 **The Blessed Lord said :**

Blessed be thou ! I will declare to thee My divine glory by its chief characteristics, O best of the Kurus ; there is no end to details of Me.

20 I, O Guḍākes'a, am the SELF, seated in the heart of all beings ; I am the beginning, the middle, and also the

21 end of all beings. Of the Ādityas I am
Viṣṇu ; of radiances the glorious sun ;
I am Marīci of the Maruts ; of the
22 asterisms the Moon am I. Of the
Vedas I am the Sāma-Veda ; I am
Vāsava of the Shining Ones ; and of
the senses I am the mind[1] ; I am of
23 living beings the intelligence[2]. And of
the Rudras[3] S'aṅkara am I ; Vittes'a
of the Yakṣas and Rākṣasas[4] ; and
of the Vasus[3] I am Pāvaka ; Meru of
24 high mountains am I. And know Me,
O Pārtha, of household priests the
chief, Bṛhaspati ; of generals I am

[1] Manas.
[2] Cetana.
[3] Celestial Beings.
[4] Semi-human beings.

25 Skanda; of lakes I am the ocean. Of
the great Ṛṣis Bhṛgu; of speech I
am the one syllable[1]; of sacrifices I
am the sacrifice of silent repetitions[2];
of immovable things the Himālaya,
26 As'vattha of all trees; and of divine
Ṛṣis Nārada; of Gandharvas[3] Citra-
ratha; of the perfected the Muni
27 Kapila. Uccais'ravas of horses know
me, nectar[4]-born; Airāvata of lordly
elephants, and of men the Monarch.
28 Of weapons I am the thunderbolt; of
cows I am Kāmadhuk; I am Kandarpa
of the progenitors; of serpents Vāsuki

[1] Om.

[2] Japa.

[3] Celestial singers.

[4] Amṛta, the nectar of immortality.

29 am I. And I am Ananta of Nāgas[1];
Varuṇa of sea-dwellers I; and of
ancestors Aryaman; Yama of governors
30 am I. And I am Prahlāda of Daityas[2];
of calculators Time am I; and of wild
beasts I the imperial beast[3]; and Vaina-
31 teya of birds. Of purifiers I am the
wind; Rāma of warriors I; and I am
Makara of fishes; of streams the Gaṅgā
32 am I. Of creations the beginning and
the ending, and also the middle am I,
O Arjuna. Of sciences the science concerning the SELF; the speech of ora-
33 tors I. Of letters the letter A I am,

[1] Serpents, who were Teachers of Wisdom.

[2] Semi-human beings.

[3] Lion.

and the duality of a compound[1]; I
also everlasting Time; I the Supporter,
34 whose face turns everywhere. And all-
devouring Death am I, and the origin
of all to come; and of feminine qualities, fame, prosperity, speech, memory,
intelligence, constancy, forgiveness.
35 Of hymns also Bṛhatsāman; Gāyatrī of
metres am I; of months I am Mār-
36 gas'īrsa; of seasons the flowery. I
am the gambling of the cheat, and the
splendour of splendid things I; I am
victory, I am determination, and the
37 truth of the truthful I. Of the Vṛṣ-
ṇis[2] Vāsudeva am I; of the Pāṇḍavas[2]

[1] Dvandva.

[2] A family, or clan, among the Hindus.

Dhanañjaya; of the Sages[1] also I am
38 Vyāsa; of poets Us'anas the Bard. Of
rulers I am the sceptre; of those that
seek victory I am statesmanship; and
of secrets I am also silence; the knowledge of knowers am I.
39 And whatsoever is the seed of all
beings, that am I, O Arjuna; nor is
there aught, moving or unmoving, that
40 may exist bereft of Me. There is no
end of My divine powers, O Parantapa.
What has been declared is illustrative
41 of My infinite glory. Whatsoever is
glorious, good, beautiful, and mighty,
understand thou that to go forth from
42 a fragment of My splendour. But what
is the knowledge of all these details to

[1] Munis.

thee, O Arjuna ? Having pervaded this whole universe with one fragment of Myself, I remain.

Thus in the glorious Upaniṣads of the BHAGAVAD-GĪTĀ the science of the ETERNAL, the scripture of Yoga, the dialogue between S'rī Kṛṣṇa and Arjuna, the tenth discourse, entitled :

THE YOGA OF SOVEREIGNTY

ELEVENTH DISCOURSE

1 **Arjuna said:**

This word of the supreme Secret concerning
the SELF, Thou hast spoken out of compassion;
2 by this my delusion is taken away. The production and destruction of beings have been heard
by me in detail from Thee, O Lotus-eyed, and
3 also Thy imperishable greatness. O supreme
Lord,[1] even as Thou describest Thyself, O best
of beings, I desire to see Thy Form omnipotent.
4 If Thou thinkest that by me It can be seen,
O Lord, Lord of Yoga, then show me Thine
imperishable SELF.

5 **The Blessed Lord said:**

Behold, O Pārtha, a Form of Me, a hundred-
fold, a thousandfold, various in kind, divine,

[1] Īs'vara, the Creator and Ruler of a universe.

6 various in colours and shapes. Behold the
Ādityas, the Vasus, the Rudras, the two As'vins
and also the Maruts[1]; behold many marvels
7 never seen ere this, O Bhārata. Here, to-day,
behold the whole universe, movable and immovable, standing in one in My body, O Guḍā-
8 kes'a, with aught else thou desirest to see. But
verily thou art not able to behold Me with these
thine eyes; the divine eye I give unto thee.
Behold My sovereign Yoga.

9 **Sanjaya said :**

Having thus spoken, O King, the great Lord
of Yoga, Hari, showed to Pārtha His supreme
10 Form as Lord[2]. With many mouths and eyes
with many visions of marvel, with many divine
ornaments, with many upraised divine weapons
11 wearing divine necklaces and vestures, anointed

[1] Various classes of Celestial Beings.

[2] Īs'vara.

with divine unguents, the God all-marvellous,
12 boundless, with face turned everywhere. If the
splendour of a thousand suns were to blaze
out together in the sky, that might resemble
13 the glory of that Mahātmā. There Pāṇḍava
beheld the whole universe, divided into manifold
parts, standing in one in the body of the Deity
14 of Deities. Then he, Dhanañjaya, overwhelmed
with astonishment, his hair upstanding, bowed
down his head to the Shining One, and with
joined palms spake.

15 **Arjuna said:**

Within Thy Form, O god, the Gods I see,
All grades of beings with distinctive marks;
Brahmā, the Lord, upon His lotus-throne,
The Ṛṣis all, and Serpents, the divine.

16 With mouths, eyes, arms, breasts multitudinous,
I see Thee everywhere, unbounded Form.

Beginning, middle, end, nor source of Thee,
Infinite Lord, infinite Form, I find ;

17 Shining, a mass of splendour everywhere,
With discus, mace, tiara, I behold ;
Blazing as fire, as sun dazzling the gaze,
From all sides in the sky, immeasurable.

18 Lofty beyond all thought, unperishing,
Thou treasure-house supreme, all-immanent ;
Eternal Dharma's changeless Guardian, Thou ;
As immemorial Man I think of Thee.

19 Nor source, nor midst nor end ; infinite force,
Unnumbered arms, the sun and moon Thine eyes.
I see Thy face, as sacrificial fire
Blazing, its splendour burneth up the worlds.

20 By Thee alone are filled the earth, the heavens,
And all the regions that are stretched between ;

The triple worlds sink down, O mighty One,
Before Thine awful manifested Form.

21 To Thee the troops of Suras enter in,
Some with joined palms in awe invoking Thee;
Banded Maharṣis, Siddhas, cry: " All hail! "
Chanting Thy praises with resounding songs.

22 Rudras, Vasus, Sādhyas and Ādityas,
Vis'vas, the As'vins, Maruts, Ūṣmapās,
Gandharvas, Yakṣas, Siddhas, Asuras[1],
In wondering multitudes beholding Thee.

23 Thy mighty Form, with many mouths and eyes,
Long-armed, with thighs and feet innumerate,
Vast-bosomed, set with many fearful teeth,
The world see terror-struck, as also I.

[1] Names of various grades of super-physical beings.

24 Radiant, Thou touchest heaven, rainbow-hued,
With opened mouths and shining vast-orbed eyes.
My inmost self is quaking, having seen,
My strength is withered, Viṣṇu, and my peace.

25 Like Time's destroying flames I see Thy teeth,
Upstanding, spread within expanded jaws ;
Nought know I anywhere, no shelter find.
Mercy, O God ! Refuge of all the worlds !

26 The sons of Dhṛtarāṣṭra, and with them,
The multitude of all these kings of earth,
Bhiṣma, and Droṇa, Sūta's royal son,
And all the noblest warriors of our hosts.

27 Into Thy gaping mouths they hurrying rush,
Tremendous-toothed and terrible to see ;
Some caught within the grasps between Thy teeth
Are seen, their heads to powder crushed and round.

28 As river-floods impetuously rush,
Hurling their waters into ocean's lap,
So fling themselves into Thy flaming mouths,
In haste, these mighty men, these lords of earth.

29 As moths with quickened speed will headlong fly
Into a flaming light, to fall destroyed,
So also these, in haste precipitate,
Enter within Thy mouths destroyed to fall.

30 On every side, all-swallowing, fiery-tongued,
Thou lickest up mankind, devouring all;
Thy glory filleth space; the universe
Is burning, Viṣṇu, with Thy blazing rays.

31 Reveal Thy SELF; what awful Form art Thou?
I worship Thee! Have mercy, God supreme!
Thine inner Being I am fain to know;
This Thy forthstreaming Life bewilders me.

32 **The Blessed Lord said :**

Time am I, laying desolate the world,
Made manifest on earth to slay mankind!
Not one of all these warriors ranged for strife
Escapeth death ; thou shalt alone survive.

33 Therefore stand up! win for thyself renown,
Conquer thy foes, enjoy the wealth-filled realm.
By Me they are already overcome,
Be thou the outward cause, left-handed one.

34 Droṇa and Bhīṣma and Jayadratha,
Karṇa, and all the other warriors here,
Are slain by Me. Destroy them fearlessly,
Fight! thou shalt crush thy rivals in the field.

35 **Sanjaya said :**

Having heard these words of Keśava, he who weareth a diadem, with joined palms quaking and prostrating himself, spake again to Kṛṣṇa stammering with fear, casting down his face.

36 **Arjuna said**:

Hṛīṣikeśa! in Thy magnificence
Rightly the world rejoiceth, hymning Thee;
The Rākṣasas to every quarter fly
In fear; the hosts of Siddhas prostrate fall.

37 How should they otherwise? O loftiest SELF!
First Cause! Brahmā Himself less great than
Thou.
Infinite, God of Gods, home of all worlds,
Unperishing, Sat[1], Asat[2], THAT supreme!

38 First of the Gods, most ancient Man Thou art,
Supreme receptacle of all that lives;

[1] Being. [2] Non-being.

Knower and known, the dwelling-place on high;
In Thy vast Form the universe is spread.

39 Thou art Vāyu and Yama, Agni, moon,
Varuṇa, Father, Grandsire of all;
Hail, hail to Thee! a thousand times all hail!
Hail unto Thee! again, again all hail!

40 Prostrate in front of Thee, prostrate behind;
Prostrate on every side to Thee, O All.
In power boundless, measureless in strength,
Thou holdest all; then Thou Thyself art All.

41 If, thinking Thee but friend, importunate,
O Kṛṣṇa! or O Yādava! O friend!
I cried, unknowing of Thy majesty,
And careless in the fondness of my love;

42 If jesting, I irreverence showed to Thee,
At play, reposing, sitting or at meals,

Alone, O sinless One, or with my friends,
Forgive my error, O Thou boundless One.

43 Father of worlds, of all that moves and stands,
Worthier of reverence than the Guru's self,
There is none like to Thee. Who passeth Thee?
Pre-eminent Thy power in all the worlds.

44 Therefore I fall before Thee; with my body
I worship as is fitting; bless Thou me.
As father with the son, as friend with friend,
With the beloved as lover, bear with me.

45 I have seen that which none hath seen before,
My heart is glad, yet faileth me for fear;
Show me, O God, Thine other Form again—
Mercy, O God of Gods, home of all worlds—

46 Diademed, mace and discus in Thy hand.
Again I fain would see Thee as before;

Put on again Thy four-armed shape, O Lord,
O thousand-armed, of forms innumerate.

47 **The Blessed Lord said :**

Arjuna, by My favour thou hast seen
This loftiest Form by yoga's self revealed !
Radiant, all-penetrating, endless, first,
That none except thyself hath ever seen.

48 Nor sacrifice, nor Vedas, alms, nor works,
Nor sharp austerity, nor study deep,
Can win the vision of this Form for man,
Foremost of Kurus, thou alone hast seen.

49 Be not bewildered, be thou not afraid,
Because thou hast beheld this awful Form ;
Cast fear away, and let thy heart rejoice ;
Behold again Mine own familiar shape.

50 **Sanjaya said:**

Vāsudeva, having thus spoken to Arjuna, again manifested His own Form, and consoled the terrified one, the Mahātman again assuming a gentle form.

51 **Arjuna said:**

Beholding again Thy gentle human Form, O Janārdana, I am now collected, and am restored to my own nature.

52 **The Blessed Lord said:**

This Form of Mine beholden by thee is very
hard to see. Verily the Shining Ones ever
53 long to behold this Form. Nor can I be
seen as thou hast seen Me by the Vedas, nor
by austerities, nor by alms, nor by offerings;
54 but by devotion to Me alone I may thus be
perceived, Arjuna, and known and seen in

55 essence, and entered, O Parantapa. He who doeth actions for Me, whose supreme good I am, My devotee, freed from attachment, without hatred of any being, he cometh unto Me, O Pāṇḍava.

Thus in the glorious Upaniṣads of the BHAGAVAD-GĪTĀ, the science of the ETERNAL, the scripture of Yoga, the dialogue between S'rī Kṛṣṇa and Arjuna, the eleventh discourse, entitled :

THE YOGA OF THE VISION OF THE UNIVERSAL FORM

TWELFTH DISCOURSE

1 **Arjuna said:**

Those devotees who ever harmonized worship Thee, and those also who worship the Indestructible, the Unmanifested, who of these is the more learned in yoga?

2 **The Blessed Lord said:**

They who with mind[1] fixed on Me, ever harmonized worship Me, with faith supreme endowed, these in My opinion, are best in yoga.

[1] Manas.

3 They who worship the Indestructible,
the Ineffable, the Unmanifested, Omnipresent, and Unthinkable, the Unchang-
4 ing, Immutable, Eternal, restraining
and subduing the senses, regarding
everything equally, in the welfare of all
rejoicing, these also come unto Me.
5 The difficulty of those whose minds are
set on the Unmanifested is greater; for
the path of the Unmanifested is hard
for the embodied to reach.

6 Those verily who, renouncing all
actions in Me and intent on Me, worship meditating on Me, with whole-
7 hearted yoga, these I speedily lift up
from the ocean of death and existence, O
Pārtha, their minds [1] being fixed on Me.

[1] Cetas.

8 Place thy mind[1] in [me, into Me let
thy Reason[2] enter; then without doubt
9 thou shalt abide in Me hereafter. And
if thou art not able firmly to fix thy
mind[3] on Me, then by the yoga of practice seek to reach Me, O Dhanañjaya.
10 If also thou art not equal to constant
practice, be intent on my service; performing actions for My sake, thou shalt
11 attain perfection. If even to do this thou
hast not strength, then, taking refuge
in union with Me, renounce all fruit of
12 action with the self controlled. Better
indeed is wisdom than constant practice;
than wisdom, meditation is better;

[1] Manas.

[2] Buddhi.

[3] Citta.

than meditation, renunciation of the
fruit of action; on renunciation follows
peace.
13 He who beareth no ill-will to any
being, friendly and compassionate, without attachment and egoism, balanced in
14 pleasure and pain, and forgiving, ever
content, harmonious with the self controlled, resolute, with mind[1] and Reason[2] dedicated to Me, he, My devotee,
15 is dear to Me. He from whom the
world doth not shrink away, who doth
not shrink away from the world, freed
from the anxieties of joy, anger, and
16 fear, he is dear to Me. He who wants
nothing, is pure, expert, passionless,

[1] Manas.

[2] Buddhi.

untroubled, renouncing every undertaking, he, My devotee, is dear to Me.
17 He who neither loveth nor hateth, nor
grieveth, nor desireth, renouncing good
and evil, full of devotion, he is dear to
18 Me. Alike to foe and friend, and also
in fame and ignominy, alike in cold and
heat, pleasures and pains, destitute of
19 attachment, taking equally praise and
reproach, silent, wholly content with
what cometh, homeless, firm in mind,
full of devotion, that man is dear to
Me.

20 They verily who partake of this life-
giving wisdom [1] as taught herein, endued
with faith, I their supreme Object,

[1] Amṛta-Dharma.

devotees, they are surpassingly dear to Me.

Thus in the glorious Upaniṣads of the BHAGAVAD-GĪTĀ, the science of the ETERNAL, the scripture of Yoga, the dialogue between S'rī Kṛṣṇa and Arjuna, the twelfth discourse, entitled :

THE YOGA OF DEVOTION

THIRTEENTH DISCOURSE

Arjuna said :

Matter and Spirit [1], even the Field and the Knower of the Field, wisdom and that which ought to be known, these I fain would learn, O Keśava.[2]

1 **The Blessed Lord said :**

This body, son of Kuntī, is called the
Field ; that which knoweth it is called
the Knower of the Field by the Sages.
2 Understand Me as the Knower of the
Field in all Fields, O Bhārata. Wisdom
as to the Field and the Knower of the

[1] Prakṛti and Puruṣa.

[2] This verse is omitted in many editions.

Field, that in My opinion is the
3 Wisdom. What that Field is and of
what nature, how modified, and whence
it is, and what He[1] is and what His
powers, hear that now briefly from Me.
4 Ṛṣis have sung in manifold ways,
in many various chants, and in decisive
Brahma-sūtra verses[2], full of reasonings.
5 The great Elements, individuality[3],
Reason[4] and also the Unmanifested,
the ten senses and the one, and the
6 five pastures of the senses[5]; desire,

[1] Kṣetrajña, the Knower of the Field.

[2] Short terse sayings, concerning the ETERNAL.

[3] Ahaṅkāra.

[4] Buddhi.

[5] The five organs of knowledge, or senses, the five organs of action, the mind, and the objects cognized by each of the five senses.

aversion, pleasure, pain, combination[1], intelligence, firmness ; these, briefly described, constitute the Field and its modifications.

7 Humility, unpretentiousness, harmlessness, forgiveness, rectitude, service of the teacher, purity, steadfastness,
8 self-control, dispassion towards the objects of the senses, and also absence of egoism, insight into the pain and evil of birth, death, old age and sick-
9 ness, unattachment, absence of self-identification with son, wife or home, and constant balance of mind in wished-
10 for and unwished-for events, unflinching devotion to Me by yoga, without other object, resort to sequestered

[1] The body.

places, absence of enjoyment in the
11 company of men, constancy in the
Wisdom of the Self,[1] understanding of
the object of essential wisdom; that is
declared to be the Wisdom; all against
it is ignorance.
12 I will declare that which ought to be
known, that which being known immortality is enjoyed—the beginningless
supreme ETERNAL, called neither being
13 nor non-being. Everywhere THAT hath
hands and feet, everywhere eyes, heads,
and mouths; all-hearing, He dwelleth in
14 the world, enveloping all; shining with
all sense-faculties without any senses;
unattached supporting everything; and

[1] Adhyātma; see vii, 29.

free from qualities[1] enjoying qualities;[1]
15 without and within all beings, immovable and also movable; by reason of His subtlety imperceptible; at hand
16 and far away is THAT. Not divided amid beings, and yet seated distributively; THAT is to be known as the supporter of beings; He devours and
17 He generates. THAT, the Light of all lights, is said to be beyond darkness; Wisdom, the Object of Wisdom, by Wisdom to be reached, seated in the
18 hearts of all. Thus the Field, Wisdom and the Object of Wisdom, have been briefly told. My devotee, thus knowing, enters into My being.

[1] Guṇas.

19 Know thou that Matter[1] and Spirit[2]
are both without beginning; and know
thou also that modifications and quali-
20 ties[3] are all Matter-born[1]. Matter[1] is
called the cause of the generation of
causes and effects; Spirit[2] is called the
cause of the enjoyment of pleasure and
21 pain. Spirit[2] seated in Matter[1] useth the
qualities[3] born of Matter[1]; attachment
to the qualities[3] is the cause of his
22 births in good and evil wombs. Supervisor and permitter, supporter, enjoyer,
the great Lord, and also the supreme
SELF; thus is styled in this body the
supreme Spirit[2]. He who thus knoweth

[1] Prakṛti.

[2] Puruṣa.

[3] Guṇas.

Spirit[1] and Matter[2] with its qualities,[3]
in whatsoever condition he may be, he
shall not be born again.

24 Some by meditation behold the SELF
in the self by the SELF; others by the
Sāṅkhya Yoga, and others by the Yoga
25 of Action, others also, ignorant of this,
having heard of it from others, worship;
and these also cross beyond death,
adhering to what they had heard.

26 Whatsoever creature is born, immo-
bile or mobile, know thou, O best of
the Bhāratas, that it is from the union
between the Field and the Knower of
27 the Field. Seated equally in all beings,

[1] Puruṣa.

[2] Prakṛti.

[3] Guṇas.

the supreme Lord, unperishing within
the perishing—he who thus seeth, he
28 seeth. Seeing indeed everywhere the
same Lord equally dwelling, he doth
not destroy the SELF by the self, and
thus treads the highest Path.
29 He who seeth that Matter[1] verily
performeth all actions, and that the
30 SELF is actionless, he seeth. When he
perceiveth the diversified existence of
beings as rooted in One, and spreading
forth from it, then he reacheth the ETER-
31 NAL. Being beginningless and without
qualities[2], the imperishable supreme
SELF, though seated in the body, O
Kaunteya, worketh not nor is affected.

[1] Prakṛti.

[2] Guṇas.

32 As the omnipresent ether is not
affected, by reason of its subtlety, so
seated everywhere in the body the SELF
33 is not affected. As the one sun illumineth the whole earth, so the Lord of
the Field illumineth the whole Field,
34 O Bhārata. They who by the eyes of
Wisdom perceive this difference between the Field and the Knower of
the Field, and the liberation of beings
from Matter[1], they go to the Supreme.

Thus in the glorious Upaniṣads of the BHAGAVAD-GĪTĀ, the science of the ETERNAL, the scripture of Yoga, the dialogue between S′ri Kṛṣṇa and Arjuna, the thirteenth discourse, entitled :

THE YOGA OF THE DISTINCTION BETWEEN THE FIELD AND THE KNOWER OF THE FIELD

[1] Prakṛti.

FOURTEENTH DISCOURSE

1 **The Blessed Lord said:**

I will again proclaim that supreme Wisdom, of all wisdom the best, which having known, all the Sages[1] have gone hence to the supreme Perfection.

2 Having taken refuge in this Wisdom and being assimilated to My own nature, they are not re-born even in the emanation of a universe, nor are disquieted in the dissolution.

3 My womb is the great ETERNAL; in that I place the germ; thence cometh the birth of all beings, O

[1] Munis.

4 Bhārata. In whatsoever wombs mortals are produced, O Kaunteya, the great ETERNAL is their womb, I their generating father.

5 Harmony[1], Motion, Inertia, such are the qualities[2], Matter-born[3]; they bind fast in the body, O great-armed one, the indestructible dweller in the body.
6 Of these Harmony, from its stainlessness, luminous and healthy, bindeth by the attachment to bliss and the attach-
7 ment to wisdom, O sinless one. Motion, the passion-nature, know thou, is the source of attachment and thirst for life, O Kaunteya, that bindeth the

[1] More strictly Rhythm.
[2] Guṇas.
[3] Prakṛti.

dweller in the body by the attachment
8 to action. But Inertia, know thou,
born of unwisdom, is the deluder of all
dwellers in the body; that bindeth by
heedlessness, indolence and sloth, O
9 Bhārata. Harmony attacheth to bliss,
Motion to action, O Bhārata. Inertia,
verily, having shrouded wisdom, attacheth on the contrary to heedlessness.

10 Now Harmony prevaileth, having
overpowered Motion and Inertia, O
Bhārata. Now Motion, having overpowered Harmony and Inertia; and
now Inertia, having overpowered Har-
11 mony and Motion. When the wisdom-
light streameth forth from all the gates
of the body, then it may be known
12 that Harmony is increasing. Greed,

outgoing energy, undertaking of actions,
restlessness, desire—these are born of
the increase of Motion, O best of the
13 Bhāratas. Darkness, stagnation and
heedlessness and also delusion—these
are born of the increase of Inertia, O
joy of the Kurus.

14 If Harmony verily prevaileth when
the embodied goeth to dissolution, then
he goeth forth to the spotless worlds of
15 the great Sages. Having gone to dissolution in Motion, he is born among
those attached to action; if dissolved
in Inertia, he is born in the wombs of
the senseless.

16 It is said the fruit of a good action is
harmonious and spotless; verily the
fruit of Motion is pain, and the fruit of

17 Inertia unwisdom. From Harmony wisdom is born, and also greed from Motion; heedlessness and delusion are
18 of Inertia and also unwisdom. They rise upwards who are settled in Harmony; the Active dwell in the midmost place; the Inert go downwards, enveloped in the vilest qualities.

19 When the Seer perceiveth no agent other than the qualities[1], and knoweth THAT which is higher than the qualities[1], he entereth into My Nature.
20 When the dweller in the body hath crossed over these three qualities[1], whence all bodies have been produced, liberated from birth, death, old age and

[1] Guṇas.

sorrow, he drinketh the nectar of immortality [1].

Arjuna said:

21 What are the marks of him who hath crossed over the three qualities [2], O Lord? How acteth he, and how doth he go beyond these three qualities [2]?

The Blessed Lord said:

22 He, O Pāṇḍava, who hateth not radiance, nor outgoing energy, nor even
delusion, when present, nor longeth
23 after them, absent; He who, seated as
a neutral, is unshaken by the qualities [2];
who saying, "The qualities [2] revolve";

[1] The Amṛta.

[2] Guṇas.

24 standeth apart immovable; balanced
in pleasure and pain, self-reliant, to
whom a lump of earth, a rock and gold
are alike, the same to loved and un-
loved, firm, the same in censure and
25 in praise, the same in honour and
ignominy, the same to friend and
foe, abandoning all undertakings—he
is said to have crossed over the
qualities[1].

26 And he who serveth Me exclusively
by the Yoga of devotion, he, crossing
beyond the qualities[1], is fit to be-
27 come the ETERNAL. For I am the
abode of the ETERNAL, and of the
indestructible nectar of immortality, of

[1] Guṇas.

immemorial righteousness[1], and of unending bliss.

Thus in the glorious Upaniṣads of the BHAGAVAD-GĪTĀ, the science of the ETERNAL, the scripture of Yoga, the dialogue between S'rī Kṛṣṇa and Arjuna, the fourteenth discourse, entitled :

THE YOGA OF SEPARATION FROM THE THREE QUALITIES

[1] Dharma.

FIFTEENTH DISCOURSE

1 **The Blessed Lord said:**
With roots above, branches below, the As'vattha is said to be indestructible; the leaves of it are hymns; he who knoweth it is a Veda-knower.
2 Downwards and upwards spread the branches of it, nourished by the qualities[1]; the objects of the senses its buds; and its roots grow downwards, the bonds of action in the world of men.
3 Nor here may be acquired knowledge of its form, nor its end, nor its origin, nor its rooting-place; this strongly rooted As'vattha having been cut down by

[1] Guṇas.

the unswerving weapon of non-attach-
4 ment that path beyond may be sought,
treading which there is no return.

I go indeed to that Primal Man,[1]
whence the ancient energy forthstream-
5 ed. Without pride and delusion, victorious over the vice of attachment,
dwelling constantly in the SELF, desire
pacified, liberated from the pairs of
opposites known as pleasure and pain,
they tread, undeluded, that indestructi-
6 ble path. Nor doth the sun lighten
there, nor moon, nor fire; having gone
thither they return not; that is My
supreme abode.

7 A portion of Mine own Self, trans-
formed in the world of life into an

[1] Puruṣa.

immortal Spirit[1], draweth round itself
the senses of which the mind[2] is the
8 sixth, veiled in Matter.[3] When the Lord
acquireth a body and when He abandoneth it, He seizeth these[4] and goeth
with them, as the wind takes fragrances
9 from their retreats. Enshrined in the
ear, the eye, the touch, the taste and
the smell, and in the mind[2] also, He
10 enjoyeth the objects of the senses. The
deluded do not perceive Him when He
departeth or stayeth, or enjoyeth, swayed by the qualities[5]; the wisdom-eyed

[1] Jīva, a life, individualized from the Universal Spirit.

[2] Manas.

[3] Prakṛti.

[4] The senses and the mind.

[5] Guṇas.

11 perceive. Yogīs also, struggling, perceive Him, established in the SELF; but though struggling, the unintelligent perceive Him not, their selves untrained.

12 That splendour issuing from the sun that enlighteneth the whole world, that which is in the moon and in fire, that splendour know as from Me.
13 Permeating the soil, I support beings by my vital energy, and having become the delicious Soma[1] I nourish all plants.
14 I, having become the Fire of Life[2], take possession of the bodies of breathing

[1] "Having become the watery moon" is the accepted translation. Soma is a liquid, drawn from the Soma-plant, "Having become sap" is a probable translation.

[2] Vais'vānara.

things, and united with the life-breaths [1] I. digest the four kinds of food.
15 And I am seated in the hearts of all, and from Me memory and wisdom and their absence. And that which is to be known in all the Vedas am I; and I indeed the Veda-knower and the author of the Vedānta.
16 There are two Energies [2] in this world, the destructible and the indestructible; the destructible is all beings, the unchanging is called the indestructible.
17 The highest Energy [2] is verily Another, declared as the supreme SELF, He who pervading all sustaineth the three worlds, the indestructible Lord.

[1] Prāṇa and Apāna.

[2] Puruṣa.

18 Since I excel the destructible, and am
more excellent also than the indestructible, in the world and in the Veda
I am proclaimed the Supreme Spirit.[1]
19 He who undeluded knoweth Me thus
as the Supreme Spirit[1], he, all-know-
ing, worshippeth Me with his whole
20 being, O Bhārata. Thus by Me this
most secret teaching hath been told, O
sinless one. This known, he hath become illuminated, and hath finished his
work, O Bhārata.

Thus in the glorious Upaniṣads of the BHAGAVAD-GĪTĀ the science of the ETERNAL, the scripture of Yoga, the dialogue between S'rī Kṛṣṇa and Arjuna, the fifteenth discourse, entitled:

THE YOGA OF ATTAINING THE SUPREME SPIRIT

[1] Puruṣottama, the highest Puruṣa.

SIXTEENTH DISCOURSE

1 Fearlessness, cleanness of life, steadfastness in the Yoga of wisdom, almsgiving, self-restraint and sacrifice and study of the Scriptures, austerity
2 and straightforwardness, harmlessness, truth, absence of wrath, renunciation, peacefulness, absence of crookedness, compassion to living beings, uncovetousness, mildness, modesty, absence of
3 fickleness, vigour, forgiveness, fortitude, purity, absence of envy and pride— these are his who is born with the divine properties, O Bhārata.

4 Hypocrisy, arrogance and conceit, wrath and also harshness and unwisdom are his who is born, O, Pārtha, with demoniacal[1] properties.

5 The divine properties are deemed to be for liberation, the demoniacal for bondage. Grieve not, thou art born with divine properties, O Pāṇḍava.

6 Twofold is the animal creation in this world, the divine and the demoniacal: the divine hath been described at length: hear from Me, O Pārtha, the demoniacal.

7 Demoniacal men know neither right energy nor right abstinence; nor purity nor even propriety, nor truth is in them.

[1] Āsuric; the Asuras were the enemies of the Suras, or Gods.

8 "The universe is without truth, without basis," they say, "without a God[1];
brought about by mutual union, and
9 caused by lust and nothing else." Holding this view, these ruined selves of
small understanding[2], of fierce deeds,
come forth as enemies for the destruc-
10 tion of the world. Surrendering themselves to insatiable desires, possessed
with vanity, conceit and arrogance,
holding evil ideas through delusion, they
engage in action with impure resolves.
11 Giving themselves over to unmeasured
thought whose end is death, regarding
the gratification of desires as the highest,
12 feeling sure that this is all, held in

[1] Īs'vara; the ruler of the universe.

[2] Buddhi.

bondage by a hundred ties of expectation, given over to lust and anger, they strive to obtain by unlawful means hoards of wealth for sensual enjoyments.

13 "This to-day by me hath been won,
that purpose I shall gain; this wealth
is mine already, and also this shall
14 be mine in future. I have slain this
enemy, and others also I shall slay. I
15 am the Lord, I am the enjoyer, I
am perfect, powerful, happy; I am
wealthy, well-born; what other is there
that is like unto me? I will sacrifice, I
will give alms, I will rejoice." Thus
16 deluded by unwisdom, bewildered by
numerous thoughts, enmeshed in the

web of delusion, addicted to the gratification of desire, they fall downwards into a foul hell.

17 Self-glorifying, stubborn, filled with the pride and intoxication of wealth, they perform lip-sacrifices for ostentation, contrary to scriptural ordinance.
18 Given over to egoism, power, insolence,
lust and wrath, these malicious ones
hate Me in the bodies of others and in
19 their own. These haters, evil, pitiless,
vilest among men in the world, I ever
throw down into demoniacal wombs,
20 Cast into demoniacal wombs, deluded
birth after birth, attaining not to Me,
O Kaunteya, they sink into the lowest
depths.

21 Triple is the gate of this hell,
destructive of the self—lust, wrath,
and greed, therefore let man renounce
22 these three. A man liberated from
these three gates of darkness, O son
of Kuntī, accomplisheth his own welfare, and thus reacheth the highest
goal.
23 He who having cast aside the ordinances of the Scriptures, followeth the
promptings of desire, attaineth not to
perfection, nor happiness, nor the high-
24 est goal. Therefore let the Scriptures
be thy authority, in determining what
ought to be done, or what ought not to
be done. Knowing what hath been
declared by the ordinances of the

Scriptures, thou oughtest to work in this world.

Thus in the glorious Upaniṣads of the BHAGAVAD-GĪTĀ, the science of the ETERNAL, the scripture of Yoga, in the dialogue between S'ri Kṛṣṇa and Arjuna, the sixteenth discourse, entitled :

THE YOGA OF DIVISION BETWEEN THE DIVINE AND THE DEMONIACAL

SEVENTEENTH DISCOURSE

1 **Arjuna said:**

Those that sacrifice full of faith[1], but casting aside the ordinances of the Scriptures, what is verily their condition, O Kṛṣṇa? Is it one of Purity, Passion, or Darkness[2]?

2 **The Blessed Lord said:**

Threefold is by nature the inborn faith of the embodied—pure, passionate, and dark. Hear thou of these.

[1] S'raddhā.

[2] The three qualities, Sattva, Rajas, Tamas, are here used in their moral correspondences, and are therefore translated as Purity, Passion, and Darkness.

3 The faith of each is shaped to his own nature, O Bhārata. The man consists of his faith [1]; that which his faith is, he is even that.

4 Pure men worship the Shining Ones; the passionate the gnomes and giants [2]; the others, the dark folk, worship ghosts and troops of nature-spirits [3].

5 The men who perform severe austerities, unenjoined by the Scriptures, wedded to vanity and egoism, impelled by the force of their desires and passions,

[1] That is, the man's faith shows what is the man's character.

[2] Yakṣas, gnomes, are the servants of the Lord of Wealth, *i.e.*, are connected with metals; Rākṣasas, giants, or Titans, were the gigantic inhabitants of Atlantis, versed in magic and sorcery.

[3] Prètās, ghosts, are departed men, while Bhūtas, nature-spirits, are of a somewhat goblin-like type.

6 unintelligent, tormenting the aggre-
gated elements forming the body, and
Me also, seated in the inner body,
know these demoniacal in their resolves.
7 The food also which is dear to each
is threefold, as also sacrifice, austerity
and almsgiving. Hear thou the distinc-
8 tion of these. The foods that augment
vitality, energy, vigour, health, joy and
cheerfulness, delicious, bland, substan-
tial and agreeable, are dear to the pure.
9 The passionate desire foods that are
bitter, sour, saline, over-hot, pungent,
dry and burning, and which produce
10 pain, grief and sickness. That which
is stale and flat, putrid and corrupt,
leavings also and unclean, is the food
dear to the dark.

11 The sacrifice which is offered by men without desire for fruit, as enjoined by the ordinances, under the firm belief that sacrifice is a duty, that is pure.
12 The sacrifice offered with a view verily to fruit, and also indeed for self-glorification, O best of the Bhāratas; know
13 thou that to be of passion. The sacrifice contrary to the ordinances, without distributing food, devoid of words of power[1] and without gifts[2], empty of faith, is said to be of darkness.

14 Worship given to the Shining Ones, to the twice-born, to the Teachers[3] and to the wise, purity, straightforwardness,

[1] Mantras.

[2] To the officiating priests.

[3] Gurus.

continence and harmlessness, are called
15 the austerity of the body. Speech
causing no annoyance, truthful, pleasant
and beneficial, the practice of the study
of the Scriptures, are called the auster-
16 ity of speech. Mental happiness,
equilibrium, silence, self-control, purity
of nature—this is called the austerity
17 of the mind[1]. This threefold austerity,
performed by men with the utmost
faith, without desire for fruit, harmoni-
18 zed, is said to be pure. The austerity which is practised with the
object of gaining respect, honour and
worship, and for ostentation, is said to
be of passion, unstable and fleeting.
19 That austerity done under a deluded

[1] Manas.

understanding, with self-torture, or with the object of destroying another, that is declared of darkness.

20 That alms given to one who does nothing in return, believing that a gift ought to be made, in a fit place and time, to a worthy person, that alms is
21 accounted pure. That given with a view to receiving in return, or looking for fruit again, or grudgingly, that alms
22 is accounted of passion. That alms given at unfit place and time, and to unworthy persons, disrespectfully and contemptuously, that is declared of darkness.

23 "AUM TAT SAT," this has been considered to be the threefold designation of the ETERNAL. By that were

ordained of old Brāhmaṇas, Vedas and
24 sacrifices. Therefore with the pronunciation of "AUM" the acts of sacrifice,
gift and austerity as laid down in the
ordinances are always commenced by
25 the knowers of the ETERNAL. With
the pronunciation of "TAT" and without aiming at fruit are performed the
various acts of sacrifice, austerity and
26 gift, by those desiring liberation. "SAT"
is used in the sense of reality and good-
ness; likewise, O Pārtha, the word
"SAT" is used in the sense of a good
27 work. Steadfastness in sacrifice, austerity and gift is also called "SAT," and
an action for the sake of the Supreme[1]
is also named "Sat".

[1] TAT.

28 Whatsoever is wrought without faith, oblation, gift, austerity, or other deed, "Asat" it is called, O Pārtha; it is nought, here or hereafter.

Thus in the glorious Upaniṣads of the BHAGAVAD-GĪTĀ, the science of the ETERNAL, the scripture of Yoga, the dialogue between S'rī Kṛṣṇa and Arjuna, the seventeenth discourse, entitled:

THE YOGA OF THE DIVISION OF THREEFOLD FAITH

EIGHTEENTH DISCOURSE

1 **Arjuna said:**

I desire, O mighty-armed, to know severally the essence of renunciation[1], O Hṛṣīkes'a, and of relinquishment[2], O Kes'iniṣūdana[3].

2 **The Blessed Lord said:**

Sages have known as renunciation
the renouncing of works with desire;
the relinquishing of the fruit of all
actions is called relinquishment by the
3 wise. "Action should be relinquished

[1] Saṁnyāsa.

[2] Tyāga.

[3] Slayer of Kes'i, a demon.

as an evil[1]," declare some thoughtful
men; "acts of sacrifice, gift and austerity should not be relinquished," say
4 others. Hear my conclusions as to that
relinquishment, O best of the Bhāratas;
since relinquishment, O tiger of men,
has been explained as threefold.
5 Acts of sacrifice, gift and austerity
should not be relinquished, but should
be performed; sacrifice, gift and also
austerity are the purifiers of the intel-
6 ligent. But even these actions should
be done leaving aside attachment and
fruit, O Pārtha; that is my certain and
7 best belief. Verily renunciation of
actions that are prescribed is not
proper; the relinquishment thereof

[1] Some read: "because it is evil."

from delusion is said to be of darkness.
8 He who relinquisheth an action from
fear of physical suffering, saying "Painful," thus performing a passionate relinquishment, obtaineth not the fruit of
9 relinquishment. He who performeth a
prescribed action, saying, "It ought to
be done," O Arjuna, relinquishing
attachment and also fruit, that re-
10 linquishment is regarded as pure. The
relinquisher pervaded by purity, in-
telligent and with doubts cut away,
hateth not unpleasurable action nor is
11 attached to pleasurable. Nor indeed
can embodied beings completely re-
linquish action; verily he who relinquisheth the fruit of action he is said
12 to be a relinquisher. Good, evil and

mixed—threefold is the fruit of action hereafter for the non-relinquisher; but there is none ever for the renouncer.
13 These five causes, O mighty-armed, learn of Me as declared in the Sāṅkhya system for the accomplishment of all
14 actions: the body, the actor, the various organs, the diverse kinds of energies, and the presiding deities also,
15 the fifth. Whatever action a man performeth by his body, speech and mind[1], whether right or the reverse these five
16 are the cause thereof. That being so, he verily who—owing to untrained Reason[2]—looketh on his SELF, which is isolated, as the actor, he, of perverted

[1] Manas.

[2] Buddhi.

17 intelligence, seeth not. He who is free
from the egoistic notion, whose Reason [1]
is not affected, though he slay these
peoples, he slayeth not, nor is bound.
18 Knowledge, the knowable and the
knower, the threefold impulse to action;
the organ, the action, the actor, the
19 threefold constituents of action. Knowledge, action and actor in the category
of qualities [2] are also said to be severally
threefold, from the difference of qualities [2]; hear thou duly these also.
20 That by which one indestructible
Being is seen in all beings, inseparate
in the separated, know thou that know-
21 ledge as pure. But that knowledge

[1] Buddhi.
[2] Guṇas.

which regardeth the several manifold
existences in all beings as separate, that
knowledge know thou as of passion.
22 While that which clingeth to each one
thing as if it were the whole, without
reason, without grasping the reality,
narrow, that is declared to be dark.
23 An action which is ordained, done by
one undesirous of fruit, devoid of
attachment, without love or hate, that
24 is called pure. But that action that is
done by one longing for desires, or
again with egoism, or with much effort,
25 that is declared to be passionate. The
action undertaken from delusion, without regard to capacity and to conse-
quences—loss and injury to others—
that is declared to be dark.

26 Liberated from attachment, not egoistic, endued with firmness and confidence, unchanged by success or failure,
27 that actor is called pure. Impassioned, desiring to obtain the fruit of actions, greedy, harmful, impure, moved by joy and sorrow, such an actor is pronounced
28 passionate. Discordant, vulgar, stubborn, cheating, malicious, indolent, despairful, procrastinating, that actor is called dark.

29 The division of Reason [1] and of firmness also, threefold according to the qualities [2], hear thou related, unreservedly and severally, O Dhanañjaya.
30 That which knoweth energy and

[1] Buddhi.

[2] Guṇas.

abstinence, what ought to be done, and
what ought not to be done, fear and
fearlessness, bondage and liberation,
31 that Reason[1] is pure, O Pārtha. That
by which one understandeth awry Right
and Wrong[2] and also what ought to be
done and what ought not to be done,
that Reason[1], O Pārtha, is passionate.
32 That which, enwrapped in darkness,
thinketh wrong[3] to be right[4] and seeth
all things subverted, that Reason, O
Pārtha, is of darkness.
33 The unwavering firmness by which,
through Yoga, one restraineth the

[1] Buddhi.

[2] Dharma and Adharma, Right and Wrong in the widest sense, law and lawlessness.

[3] Adharma.

[4] Dharma.

activity of the mind[1], of the life-breaths
and of the sense-organs, that firmness,
34 O Pārtha, is pure. But the firmness,
O Arjuna, by which, from attachment
desirous of fruit, one holdeth fast duty[2],
desire and wealth, that firmness, O
35 Pārtha, is passionate. That by which
one from stupidity doth not abandon
sleep, fear, grief, despair, and also
vanity, that firmness, O Pārtha, is
dark.

36 And now the threefold kinds of
pleasure hear thou from Me, O bull of
the Bhāratas. That in which one by
practice rejoiceth, and which putteth
37 an end to pain; which at first is as

[1] Manas.

[2] Dharma.

venom but in the end is as nectar; that pleasure is said to be pure, born of the blissful knowledge of the SELF.

38 That which from the union of the senses with their objects at first is as nectar, but in the end is like venom, that pleasure is accounted passionate.

39 That pleasure which both at first and afterwards is delusive of the self, arising from sleep, indolence and heedlessness, that is declared dark.

40 There is not an entity, either on the earth or again in heaven among the Shining Ones, that is liberated from these three qualities[1], born of Matter[2].

41 Of Brāhmaṇas, Kṣattriyas, Vaiśyas

[1] Guṇas.

[2] Prakṛti.

and S'ūdras, O Parantapa, the duties[1]
have been distributed, according to the
qualities[2] born of their own natures.
42 Serenity, self-restraint, austerity, purity,
forgiveness and also uprightness, wisdom, knowledge, belief in God, are
the Brāhmaṇa duty[1], born of his own
43 nature. Prowess, splendour, firmness,
dexterity, and also not flying from
battle, generosity, the nature of a ruler,
are the Kṣattriya duty[1], born of his
44 own nature. Ploughing, protection of
kine, and trade are the Vais'ya duty[1],
born of his own nature. Action of the
nature of service is the S'ūdra duty[1],
born of his own nature.

[1] Karma; it is action arising from the nature fashioned by past thoughts and desires.

[2] Guṇas.

45 Man reacheth perfection by each
being intent on his own duty[1]. Listen
thou how perfection is won by him who
46 is intent on his own duty[1]. He from
whom is the emanation of beings, by
whom all this is pervaded, by worshipping Him in his own duty[1] a man
47 winneth perfection. Better is one's
own duty[2] though destitute of merits
than the well-executed duty[2] of another.
He who doeth the duty[2] laid down by
48 his own nature incurreth not sin. Congenital duty[1], O son of Kuntī, though
defective, ought not to be abandoned.

[1] Karma.

[2] Dharma. There is a subtle difference in these words, here used almost interchangeably. Karma arises from the past; Dharma also so arises, but implies also the law by which the next step in evolution is made.

All undertakings indeed are clouded by
49 defects as fire by smoke. He whose
Reason[1] is everywhere unattached, the
self subdued, dead to desires, he goeth
by renunciation to the supreme perfection of freedom from obligation[2].

50 How he who hath attained perfection
obtaineth the ETERNAL, that highest
state of wisdom, learn thou from Me
51 only succinctly, O Kaunteya. United
to the Reason[1], purified, controlling
the self by firmness, having abandoned
sound and the other objects of the
senses, having laid aside passion and
52 malice, dwelling in solitude, abstemious, speech, body and mind[3] subdued,

[1] Buddhi.
[2] Karma.
[3] Manas.

constantly fixed in meditation and yoga[1], taking refuge in dispassion,
53 having cast aside egoism, violence, arrogance, desire, wrath, covetousness, selfless and peaceful—he is fit to become the ETERNAL.
54 Becoming the ETERNAL, serene in the SELF, he neither grieveth nor desireth, the same to all beings, he obtaineth supreme devotion unto Me.
55 By devotion he knoweth Me in essence, who and what I am; having thus known Me in essence he forthwith entereth into the Supreme[2]. Though
56 ever performing all actions, taking

[1] Some read "dhyānayoga," "Yoga of meditation."

[2] THAT.

refuge in Me, by My grace he obtaineth
57 the eternal indestructible abode. Renouncing mentally all works in Me,
intent on Me, resorting to the yoga
of discrimination [1], have thy thought
58 ever on Me. Thinking on Me, thou
shalt overcome all obstacles by My
grace.

But if from egoism thou wilt not
listen, thou shalt be destroyed utterly.
59 Entrenched in egoism, thou thinkest
"I will not fight"; to no purpose
thy determination; nature will con-
60 strain thee. O son of Kuntī, bound
by thine own duty [2] born of thine own
nature, that which from delusion thou

[1] Buddhi-yoga.

[2] Karma.

desirest not to do, even that helplessly thou shalt perform.

61 The Lord dwelleth in the hearts of all beings, O Arjuna, by His illusive Power [1], causing all beings to revolve, as though mounted on a potter's wheel.

62 Flee unto Him for shelter with all thy
being, O Bhārata; by His grace thou
shalt obtain supreme peace, the ever-
63 lasting dwelling-place. Thus hath wisdom, more secret than secrecy itself, been declared unto thee by Me; having reflected on it fully, then act thou as thou listest.

64 Listen thou again to My supreme word, most secret of all; beloved art thou of Me, and steadfast of heart,

[1] Māyā.

therefore will I speak for thy benefit.
65 Merge thy mind[1] in Me, be My devotee, sacrifice to Me, prostrate thyself before Me, thou shalt come even to Me. I pledge thee My troth; thou
66 art dear to Me. Abandoning all duties[2], come unto Me alone for shelter; sorrow not, I will liberate thee from all sins.
67 Never is this to be spoken by thee to anyone who is without asceticism, nor without devotion, nor to one who desireth not to listen, nor yet to him who speaketh evil of Me.
68 He who shall declare this supreme secret among My devotees, having shown the highest devotion for Me,

[1] Manas.
[2] Dharmas.

without doubt he shall come to Me[1].
69 Nor is there any among men who
performeth dearer service to Me than
he, nor any other shall be more beloved
70 by Me on earth than he. And he who
shall study this sacred dialogue of ours.
by him I shall be worshipped with the
sacrifice of wisdom. Such is My
71 mind. The man also who, full of faith,
merely heareth it unreviling, even he,
freed from evil, obtaineth the radiant
worlds of the righteous.

72 Hath this been heard, O son of
Pṛitha, with one-pointed mind? Has
thy delusion, caused by unwisdom, been
destroyed, O Dhanañjaya?

[1] Some read "asaṁs'aya," which would be "being freed from doubts".

73 **Arjuna said:**

Destroyed is my delusion. I have gained knowledge[1] through Thy grace, O Immutable One. I am firm, my doubts have fled away. I will do according to Thy word.

74 **Sanjaya said:**

I heard this marvellous dialogue of Vāsudeva and of the great-souled Pārtha, causing my hair to stand on end;
75 by the favour of Vyāsa I listened to this secret and supreme yoga from the Lord of Yoga, Kṛṣṇa Himself speaking before mine eyes.

76 O King, remembering, remembering this marvellous and holy dialogue between Kes'ava and Arjuna, I rejoice

[1] Literally "memory".

77 again and again. Remembering, remembering, also that most marvellous form of Hari, great is my wonder, O King. I rejoice, again and again.

78 Wherever is Kṛṣṇa, Yoga's Lord, wherever is Pārtha, the archer, assured are there prosperity, victory and happiness. So I think.[1]

Thus in the glorious Upaniṣads of the BHAGAVAD-GĪTĀ, the science of the ETERNAL, the scripture of Yoga, the dialogue between S'rī Kṛṣṇa and Arjuna, the eighteenth discourse, entitled :

THE YOGA OF LIBERATION BY RENUNCIATION

Thus the BHAGAVAD-GĪTĀ hath ending.

PEACE BE TO ALL WORLDS

[1] S'rī S'aṅkarācārya's reading would run, translated : "there is prosperity, victory, happiness, and firm morality."

INDEX

INDEX

(K) denotes a title of S'rī Kṛṣṇa.
(A) a title of Arjuna.

A

H

16

S

T

U

Printed by D. V. Syamala Rau, at the Vasanta Press,
The Theosophical Society, Adyar, Madras.

Printed by D. V. Syamala Rau, at the Vasanta Press,
The Theosophical Society, Adyar, Madras.